Pop-Up Cards

OVER 50 DESIGNS FOR CARDS THAT FOLD, FLAP, SPIN, AND SLIDE

Mari Kumada

ROOST
BOOKS

BOSTON & LONDON
2012

Contents

The Story of a Boy's Birthday

Today is the boy's birthday.

He's been restless all morning.

Still not here yet . . .

Let's get the party started!

His friend has delivered his

long-awaited birthday card!

Happy Birthday!

Introduction

With cards, you don't always need to use sophisticated language.
Sometimes, just a simple, impactful word or phrase has the power
to convey everything that's important. Simplicity is especially
effective when the card is handmade. This book introduces adorable
3-D pop-up motifs that move and jump when you open the card.
The designs are all shown full-size, so that they're easy even
for beginners. As you make the designs, you may recall various
memories about the person who will receive the card, or imagine
the look of surprise on your friend's face upon opening your
card. . . . You will have a wonderful time creating handmade cards
that convey your feelings with their joyful, heartfelt delivery.

Mari Kumada

Part One

POP-UP CARDS IN SIX BASIC LESSONS

I will introduce six different basic mechanisms for creating motifs that pop up when you open the card. Each design requires only paper cutting. Just glue on the details—and your card is done! It's easy to create your own original cards by simply varying the color of the paper or the motif.

Lesson 1

HORIZONTAL-FOLD CARDS WITH 90° POP-UPS

These easy-to-make cards use straight-line cuts to make
the motif jump out. Have fun with them by choosing different
pop-up shapes or attaching various materials.

GIFT BOX

This versatile card has the power to thrill at birthdays, Christmas,
and many other occasions. The instructions are quite simple,
so even beginners can make it quickly. It's fun to vary the paper or
the ribbon color according to the person who will receive the card.

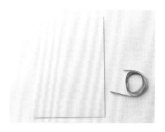

MATERIALS

1 sheet of 8½" × 11" (21.5 cm × 28 cm) Canson Mi-Teintes paper for the card base

1 piece of very thin ribbon 10" (25 cm) long

1. Cut the card base to card size (two pieces, interior and exterior) using a utility knife.

2. Temporarily attach the template to the interior piece using masking tape.

3. Cut the design through the template using a utility knife.

4. Score the fold lines by tracing them with the tip of a mechanical pencil (without any lead extended).

5. Remove the template, and fold along the scored lines. Keeping the card closed, crease the folds.

6. Glue the ribbon in place. Tie a decorative bow, and attach it to the top of the box.

7. Write your message using rubber stamps.

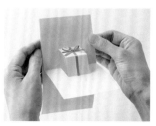

8. Glue the exterior piece to the back of the interior piece.

STRAWBERRY AND PEAR

Create cute miniature cards with dotted strawberry and pear motifs.
Use scraps of dotted fabric for the fruit. Various textures of fabric and
paper evoke different moods and produce cards with a crafty feel.
Instructions on page 82

BALLERINA DANCING ONSTAGE

The pretty ballerina dances upon the longed-for stage. An eye-popping combination of red and pink paper really turns up the loveliness factor, and the bright white lace ties the whole card together. The beautiful, feminine curves of the drop curtain only add to the effect. Instructions on page 83

Lesson 2

VERTICAL-FOLD CARDS WITH 90° POP-UPS

These cards use the trick of two folds and a cutout motif to create the pop up.
The symmetrical appeal of the finished cards makes them very charming.

HULA GIRLS

This card features girls dancing the hula in the Hawaiian
tropics and also conjures the deep marine blue of the ocean.
The hula girls look even more strikingly pretty set against
a backdrop of striped fabric.

MATERIALS

1 sheet of 8½" × 11" (21.5 cm × 28 cm) Canson Mi-Teintes paper for the card base exterior

1 sheet of 8½" × 11" (21.5 cm × 28 cm) Canson Mi-Teintes paper for the card base interior

1 piece of striped fabric 7½" × 3⅛" (19.5 cm × 8 cm)

1. Paste the fabric to the exterior of one piece of card base.

2. Cut both pieces of the card base to card size using a utility knife (now you have an interior and an exterior piece).

3. Temporarily attach the template to the interior piece using masking tape, and cut the design through the template using a utility knife.

4. Score the fold lines by tracing them with the tip of a mechanical pencil (without any lead extended).

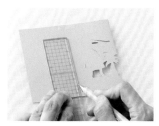

5. On the reverse side of the interior piece, score the fold line the same way.

6. Remove the template, and fold the card along the scored lines.

7. Keeping the card closed, crease the folds.

8. Paste the exterior piece to the back of the interior piece (when you do so, the cloth will appear to come from the interior).

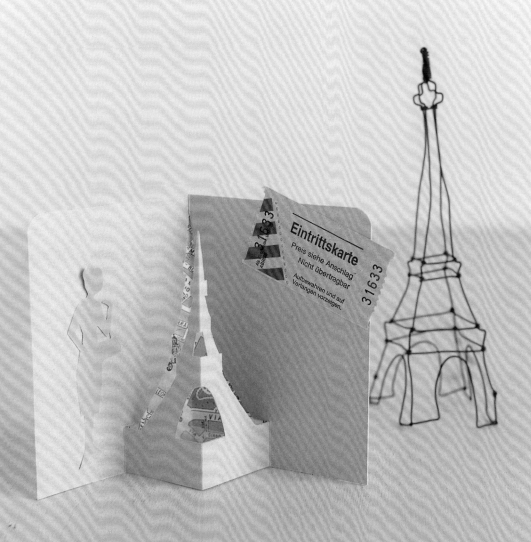

PARISIAN SCENE

Include a train ticket or a city map. . . . Brimming with travel mementos, this card exudes the spirit of traveling in a foreign country. Whether sent from abroad or presented with a souvenir gift, it's sure to please.

Instructions on page 85

RIBBON

This little card is perfect for a brief thank you or as an enclosure with a
sweet edible. The ribbon motif will enchant a young girl's heart. Finish
by adding lace or bias binding to make this sweet card even lovelier.

Instructions on page 86

Lesson 3

V-FOLD POP-UP CARDS

Open to reveal pop-up motifs in a V-fold.
Imagining how to bring 3-D shapes to life
with this design is one of the delights of
making pop-up cards.

RAINDROPS

Raindrops falling from the sky become the main
feature of this card. Make the drops nice and
round when cutting them out with a utility knife.
And because they're so small, use a toothpick to
make them really pop up out of the fold.

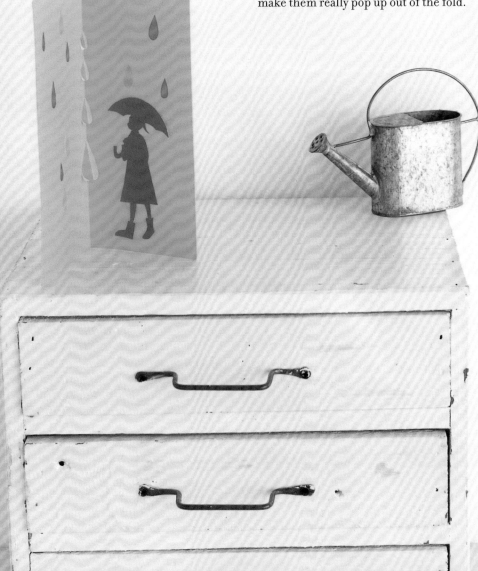

MATERIALS

1 sheet of 8½" × 11" (21.5 cm × 28 cm) Canson Mi-Teintes paper for the card base

1 piece of 8½" × 11" (21.5 cm × 28 cm) tracing paper

Color photocopies of the card motifs (girl and raindrops, page 137)

1. Cut the card base and tracing paper to card size using a utility knife.

2. Fold the card base in half. Temporarily attach the template to the folded-in-half card base using masking tape.

3. Partially cut the raindrops through the template using scissors (be careful not to cut out the entire shape).

4. Score the fold lines by tracing with the tip of a mechanical pencil (without any lead extended).

5. Remove the template, and fold the card along the scored lines. Keeping the card closed, crease the folds.

6. Paste in place the cut-out color photocopy of the girl.

7. Spreading them out evenly, paste in place the color photocopies of the raindrops.

8. Paste the tracing paper to the back of the interior piece.

TEATIME

This card makes a charming invitation to a tea party at
your home. Attach dotted fabric to the teapot on the
V-fold to evoke the warmth of a hot cuppa. It need not be
polka dots—any small pattern will work.

Instructions on page 87

THREE SISTERS

You can almost hear the voices of these close-knit sisters singing, "Un, deux, trois. . . ." The same motif makes a strikingly different impression when you use various color combinations. Which combination do you prefer?

Instructions on page 88

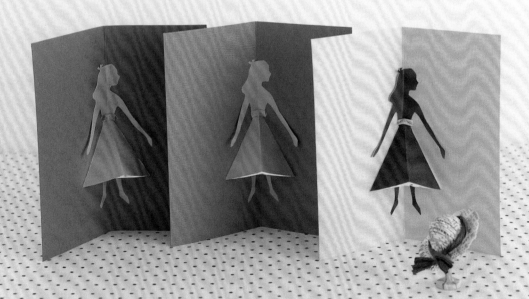

Lesson 4

POP-UP COIL CARDS

You'll wish you could see the look of surprise when your loved one opens this card. It might seem complicated to make, but the process is very simple.

SPRING'S ARRIVAL

The flowers seem to bloom all at once, and the butterfly starts to flutter. The beauty of the new season is conveyed by the pastel-colored paper. The coil is easy to make yet creates such an impact—why not challenge yourself and try it?

MATERIALS

1 sheet of 8½" × 11" (21.5 cm × 28 cm) card stock for the card base

1 sheet of 8½" × 11" (21.5 cm × 28 cm) Canson Mi-Teintes paper for the coil

1 gold bugle bead

Seed beads, as needed

Color photocopies of the card motifs (butterfly and flowers, page 138)

1. Cut the card base to card size using a utility knife.

2. Temporarily attach the template to the card base using masking tape, and trace the position of the coil's end with the tip of a mechanical pencil (without any lead extended).

3. Temporarily attach the coil template to the Mi-Teintes paper, and cut out the design through the template using scissors. Remove the template.

4. Apply glue to the tip of the coil, and attach the tip to the position traced in step 2.

5. Apply glue to other end of the coil.

6. Holding the coil in place while keeping the card closed, press down to attach it.

7. Open the card, and paste in place the color photocopies of the flower and butterflies.

8. Attach the beads using glue.

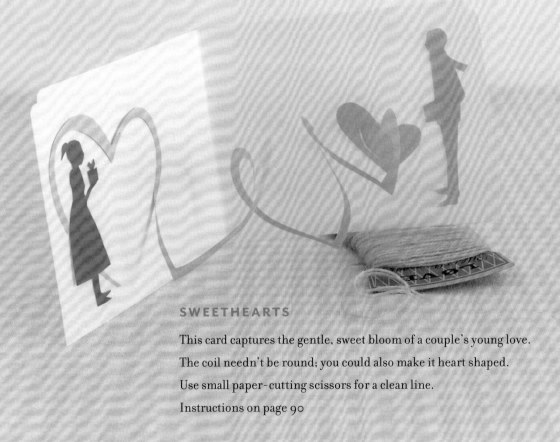

SWEETHEARTS

This card captures the gentle, sweet bloom of a couple's young love.

The coil needn't be round; you could also make it heart shaped.

Use small paper-cutting scissors for a clean line.

Instructions on page 90

THE NORTH WIND AND THE SUN

Taking a scene from the fable as its theme, this
card breathes life into the story. The thin coil,
representing the north wind as it tries to blow off
the traveler's coat, illustrates the struggle. And when
you add the fallen leaves, the gale feels even colder.
Instructions on page 91

Lesson 5

POP-UP CONE CARDS

The moment you open these cards, what seemed like a sharp edge softens into a familiar cone shape. These cards seem larger than life, so you can be sure they will make a big impression.

PIERROT HAT

Using thick, dotted paper for the hat, this card seems to make the circus pop right out of it. Give it that extra something by adding a pom-pom on top (you can find pom-poms at craft shops). This card is perfect for children's birthdays.

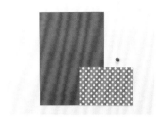

MATERIALS

1 sheet of 8½" × 11" (21.5 cm × 28 cm)
card stock for the card base

¼ sheet of 8½" × 11" (21.5 cm × 28 cm)
heavyweight paper for the hat

1 pom-pom

1. Cut the card base to card size
using a utility knife.

2. Temporarily attach the template to
the card base using masking tape, and
cut slits through the template using a
utility knife. Remove the template.

3. Temporarily attach the cone
template to the heavyweight
paper, and cut out the cone using
scissors.

4. Score the fold lines by tracing
them with the tip of a mechanical
pencil (without any lead
extended).

5. Remove the template; apply
glue to the paste overlap, and
connect the hat.

6. Insert the tabs at the base of
the cone into the slits created in
step 2.

7. Apply glue to the underside of
the tabs and paste them to the
card surface.

8. Put adhesive on the pom-pom,
and attach it to the top of the hat.

HAPPY HALLOWEEN

Add a pumpkin accent to this pointy witch's hat. Choose
paper in Halloween colors—orange and black, of course!
You could even hand these cards out along with candy to
trick-or-treaters.

Instructions on page 93

WOODLAND FRIENDS

As animals gather by the cone-shaped trees in the
forest, the chirps and cries of their conversation fill
the air. Straight out of a picture book, this card creates
a serene fantasy world.

Instructions on page 94

Lesson 6

POP-UP CUBE CARDS

Make an oblong shape, insert it in into cut slits,
and add a lid or a handle. Whatever ideas you have,
numerous motifs can be adapted into a cube card.

STRAWBERRY BASKET

Make a gift of a tiny basket filled with strawberries. Be careful to
attach the handle at just the right point; otherwise, it will stick
out when the card is closed. Experiment with the composition
by using different fruits.

MATERIALS

1 sheet of 8½" × 11" (21.5 cm × 28 cm) card stock for the card base

⅓ sheet of 8½" × 11" (21.5 cm × 28 cm) Canson Mi-Teintes paper for the basket

1 piece very thin linen ribbon measuring 6¼" (16 cm) long

Color photocopies of card motif (strawberries, page 139)

1. Cut the card base to card size using a utility knife.

2. Temporarily attach the template to the card base using masking tape, and trace the position where the basket will be attached with the tip of a mechanical pencil (without any lead extended). Remove the template.

3. Temporarily attach the basket template to the Mi-Teintes paper using masking tape, and score fold lines by tracing them with the tip of a mechanical pencil (without any lead extended). Cut out the basket using a utility knife.

4. Remove the template, and fold along the scored lines. Apply glue to the paste overlap, and connect the basket.

5. Apply glue to one of the basket's triangular paste overlaps, and attach it at the position traced on the card base. Apply glue to the other triangular paste overlap, and close the card to secure it.

6. Attach the basket handle using paste.

7. Attach the color photocopies of the strawberries using paste.

8. Attach the ribbon to the bottom of the card using adhesive.

RABBIT IN THE BRIAR

When you open this card, out hops a rabbit from the briar patch!
The high contrast of the briar's lush green and the rabbit's soft
pink is what makes this card work brilliantly. Finish it by creating
a jagged edge of grass using scissors.

Instructions on page 96

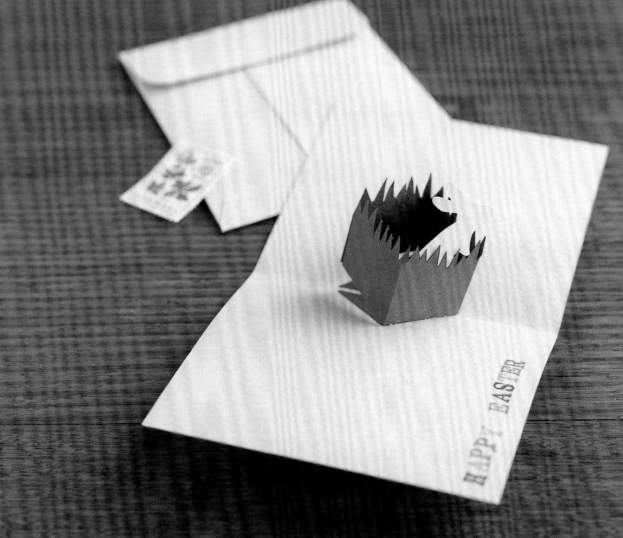

MY HOUSE

Send this card to announce a move or when throwing
a house party. It's all in the details—use assorted
fabric for the roof, and cut out the windows.
Decorate it just like your own home!

Instructions on page 97

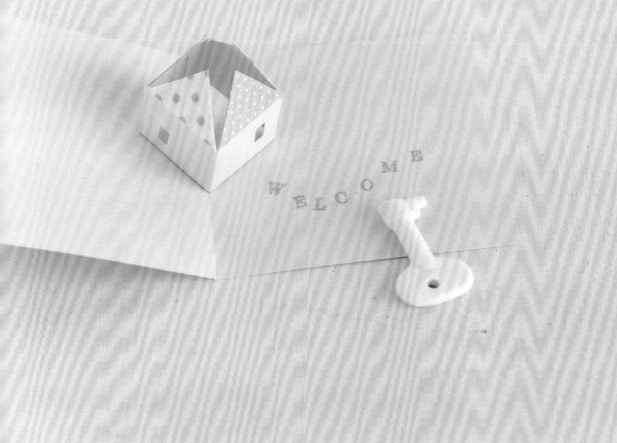

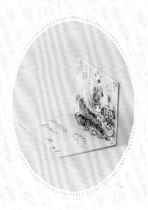

Pop-up Card Memories

The other day, I was trying to organize things in my home when I came across an old box labeled "Treasure Chest." I opened the box with anticipation and found a hodgepodge of beloved items inside. Among them, I discovered the first pop-up card I ever received. The card had an outdated joke about a centipede. Nevertheless, the pop-up legs still seemed new, springing out using the V-fold technique, and I was delighted all over again. Honestly, I don't remember much at all about receiving the card (my apologies to the aunt who gave it to me). But, I had placed it in my treasure chest, so it must have made me very happy and want to cherish it.

Part Two

POP-UP CARDS FOR ALL OCCASIONS

For celebrating birthdays, Christmas, Valentine's Day, weddings, and births, as well as simply expressing gratitude, let the person who will receive the card inspire you to create pop-up cards that freely express what you want to say.

Greeting Card 1

BIRTHDAYS

A lavish gift is nice, but it's the thought that counts, of course. An original card clearly conveys your "Happy Birthday!" wishes.

SPECIAL DELIVERY PRESENT

The bird on this card surely brings happiness along with the gift. The untied ribbon coil is what pops up. This marvelous card will be cherished as much as any present.

Instructions on page 98

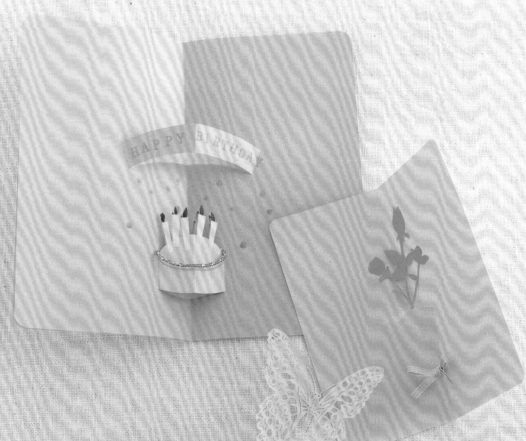

BIRTHDAY CAKE AND BOUQUET

Using these standard birthday items is all the more reason to get creative with the details. Add a sumptuous sparkling garland to the cake or an elegant silver ribbon to the bouquet to dress up the card.

Instructions on pages 99 and 100

CROWN

This gorgeously sparkling crown is perfect for such a special occasion, one that only comes once a year. Simply cutting off the top of a cone shape dramatically alters the card's impact. Dress it up in lovely finery using metallic ribbon and pearl beads.

Instructions on page 101

CHIC BUNNY

Even a cute bunny gets a chic update by opting for subtle color combinations. Pairing pale tones with rich brown paper, these cards make a distinct impression. Add elegant ribbons of fabric for even more polish.

Instructions on page 102

TO YOU...

BIRTHDAY PARTY

This card evokes the image of a proper tea parlor. Choose a delicate stripe for the card stock background, as if it were the room's wallpaper, and enhance the ambience with a feminine motif of pinks and lace.

Instructions on page 103

BIRTHDAY GIFTS

This design gives the illusion of movement by varying the sizes of the gift boxes. Each present is splendidly wrapped in different fabric. The wider you make the card, the more gift boxes you can line up!

Instructions on page 104

Greeting Card 2

CHRISTMAS

When the city dresses itself up in lights, Christmas
must be close at hand. Which kind of card will you
send to that special someone this year?

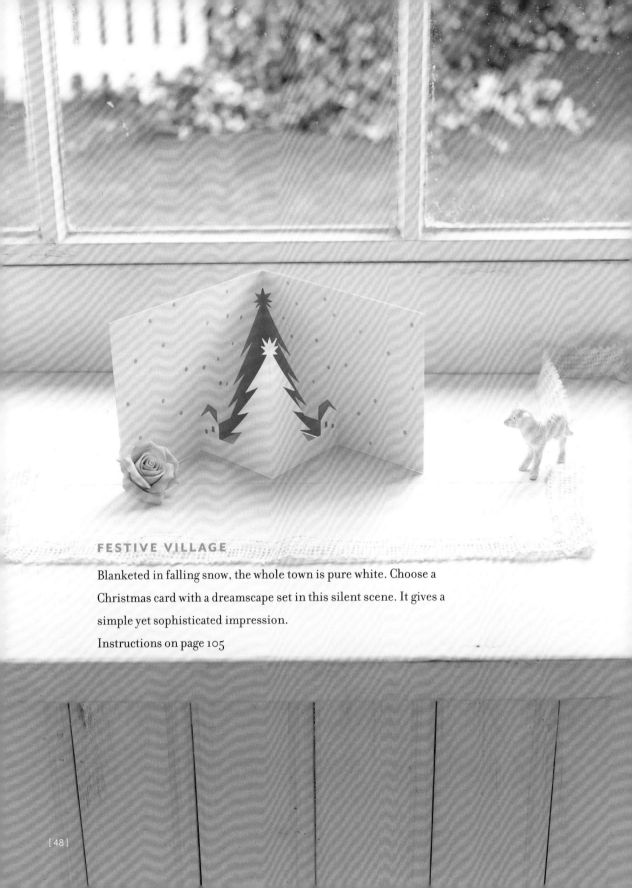

FESTIVE VILLAGE

Blanketed in falling snow, the whole town is pure white. Choose a
Christmas card with a dreamscape set in this silent scene. It gives a
simple yet sophisticated impression.

Instructions on page 105

WINTRY MOUNTAIN DEER

The sure-footed deer ambles on the wintry
mountain, and the trees watch over him. The
subdued, brown card stock as the backdrop
and restrained color accents give this card
a modern appeal. Expanding the base of the
cone makes an even greater impact.

Instructions on page 106

WINTER.

STOCKING AND SNOWMAN

Felt adds warmth and cheer to your Christmas-themed pop-up cards. You could even thread them on a string and make them into ornaments. You'll want to make these petite cards with children.

Instructions on page 107

CANDELABRA

The candelabra lit with candles makes a delicate and slender silhouette. Set it off against a background in a deeper shade of blue to emphasize the 3-D effect. Wouldn't this be perfect for an invitation to a stylish party? Instructions on page 108

SNOWFLAKE

To accentuate snow's ephemeral beauty, use only white paper. The technique is simple, but it's important to pay attention to the many detailed cuts. Start cutting from the center of the snowflake for best results. Instructions on page 109

Greeting Card 3

VALENTINE'S DAY

Delicious chocolate and an adorable card—
these two things go together when the object is love.

PETITE HEARTS

These are casual and simple cards to accompany gifts of chocolate for friends and family. All you do is cut card stock into a heart shape and make a little heart as the pop-up. Get creative with the combinations of card stock and fabric!

Instructions on page 110

HEART SURPRISE

This card uses both the V-fold and coil techniques.
With double the pop-ups, your recipient will be doubly
surprised! Using pink on pink creates a sense of harmony.
Instructions on page 111

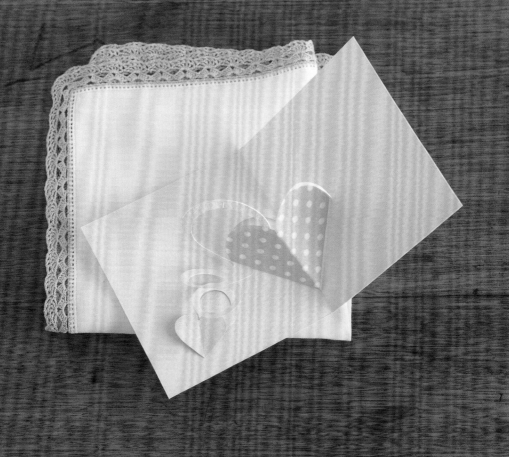

BIRDS BEARING HAPPINESS

These little birds deliver a charming heart. Choose paper patterns that complement the richness of any accompanying chocolate to create a chic motif. This card is sure to bring happiness with its undeniable thoughtfulness.

Instructions on page 112

Greeting Card 4

THANK YOU

A note of thanks shouldn't be either too overdone or too understated. Hit just the right note of gratitude with these cards that you can send right away.

CRACKER

Convey your "Thank you!" with the impact of a cracker's "Pop!" Cut and paste tiny confetti for the cracker's contents. The more colors you use, the more festive and lively the card's effect will be.

Instructions on page 113

CLOVER

This mini card takes a lucky four-leaf clover as its theme for a general note of thanks. Use a color photocopy of the clover template, cut a bit of floral wire for the stem, and paste it onto the card.

Instructions on page 114

FLUFFY SHEEP

Your recipient will proudly display this card with wool fleece glued onto the
sheep. Instead of fleece, it also looks cute when you use cotton or yarn.
Against a dark-colored background paper, the motif's silhouette really pops.

Instructions on page 115

SQUIRRELS IN LOVE

Everything but the card stock here is made of felt. One of
felt's qualities is the cozy contrast it sets up against paper.
This warm material is best used for winter cards. Feel free to
add extra craft details like buttons.

Instructions on page 116

Greeting Card 5

WEDDING AND BABY

A wedding announcement or congratulations call for a joyous card. Likewise, when a baby arrives, celebrate the birth!

CHAPEL OF LOVE

The fresh, pure white and the pretty lace create a simple, romantic image. For "something blue," choose a soft sky as background paper. The azure really sets off the cutout cross and birds.

Instructions on page 117

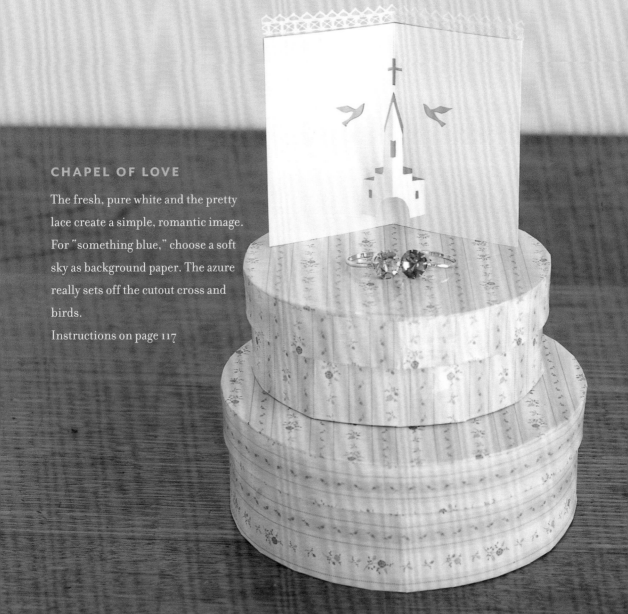

JUST MARRIED

Make this card using a double coil to celebrate the newlyweds as they leave for their honeymoon. Tastefully rendered with bursts of small, colorful flowers, this card is sure to delight the happy couple. Instructions on page 118

SWAN

Why not hand out these sweet, swan mini cards to guests gathered at the wedding reception? They're also the perfect size for place cards. Think how meaningful they would be with a few words of thanks.

Instructions on page 119

FIRST GIFT

Make baby's first card out of baby pink or baby blue paper. If the gift itself is a pair of baby booties, include a tiny felt version. A lid for the box adds detail.

Instructions on page 120

ROCKING HORSE

With a focus on soft color choices, this card features a rocking horse and a wide swath of lace. Carefully cut out the horse's legs and tail using a utility knife. Send this card to a family with a toddler learning to walk to convey your wishes for continued health and happiness.

Instructions on page 121

My Favorite Pop-up Card

I found this card in an antique variety shop that no longer
exists. The shop was located in a back alley of Yokohama's
Chinatown. Beyond its green door, secondhand American
clothes and accessories were crammed together with adorable
trinkets, and there in a corner stood this card. On the front
was printed, "Dolly and I" and "Needlebook," and when
I opened it, several young girls were happily making doll
clothes. The card also included various-sized needles and
threaders, and although its construction wasn't complicated,
I felt a slight rush of excitement when I saw it. This card would
be sure to delight, and I wanted to give it to someone myself.
It's my favorite pop-up card.

Part Three

POP-UP CARDS THAT MOVE AND SPIN

Beyond motifs or messages that pop up when you open the card, these cards use pull-tab mechanisms and rotating motifs to showcase unexpected designs. Here is a full lineup of cute cards that are so fun and heartwarming, your recipient is sure to smile.

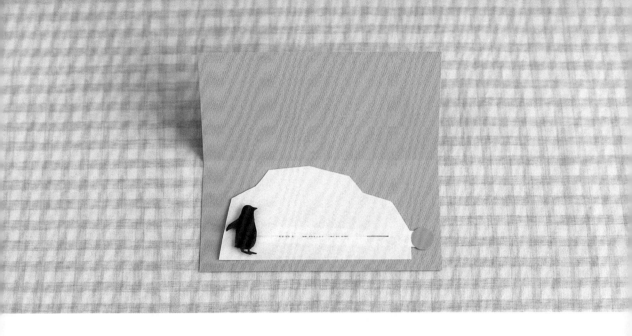

Amazing Card 1

CARDS THAT SLIDE LEFT AND RIGHT

These cards have a surprise—when you pull
on the tab mechanism, the motif moves, and
another hidden motif or message appears.

PENGUIN ON AN ICE FLOE

The penguin stands on an ice floe. Pull the tab to
reveal a message with the penguin's favorite meal:
a fish. This device will tickle the fancy of anyone
who receives the card, drawing an unexpected
giggle with its surprise message.

MATERIALS

1 sheet of 8½" × 11" (21.5 cm × 28 cm) card stock for the card base

⅓ sheet of 8½" × 11" (21.5 cm × 28 cm) card stock for the ice floe and pull tab

⅙ sheet of 8½" × 11" (21.5 cm × 28 cm) card stock for the penguin

Color photocopies of the card motifs (fish and circle, page 141)

1. Cut the card base to card size using a utility knife.

2. Temporarily attach the ice floe template to the paper using masking tape, and cut the slit for the ice floe's pull-tab mechanism through the template using a utility knife.

3. Cut out the ice floe using scissors, and remove the template.

4. Temporarily attach the pull tab template to the paper using masking tape, and cut it out using a utility knife. Remove the template, fold along the scored line, and glue together.

5. Temporarily attach the support templates for the penguin to the paper, and score fold lines by tracing them with the tip of a mechanical pencil (without any lead extended). Cut out the penguin and support using a utility knife.

6. Remove the template, and fold along the scored line of the support. Apply glue to the paste overlap, and connect the support. Apply glue to the back of the penguin, and attach it to the support.

7. Apply glue to the support, and attach it to the pull-tab mechanism through the bottom.

8. Write your message on the pull tab using rubber stamps, and glue the color photocopies of the fish and the circle to it.

9. Insert the penguin into the slit for the ice floe's pull-tab mechanism from behind.

10. Apply glue to the edges of the ice floe, and attach it to the card base.

11. Pull the tab mechanism, and adjust as needed.

Amazing Card 2

CARDS THAT FLAP

When you pull the tab mechanism, the door flaps from right to left. How exciting to pull the tab and discover what is hidden behind the flap!

HUNGRY KITTY

The kitty has her eye on the fish. Pull the tab, and you'll find the fish has been licked to the bone! Such a playful card will delight anyone who receives it. Be sure to make the pull tab using sturdy paper.

MATERIALS

1 sheet of 8½" × 11" (21.5 cm × 28 cm) card stock for the card base

Color photocopies of the card motifs (cats, plate with fish, plate with fishbone; page 141)

1. Fold the card base in half, and cut it to card size using a utility knife with the fold on the left side. (The unfolded card base will be 8" × 5½" [20 cm × 14 cm].)

2. Cut the slit for the pull-tab mechanism through the template using a utility knife. Remove the template.

3. Temporarily attach the pull-tab template to the leftover paper. Score the fold lines by tracing them with the tip of a mechanical pencil (without any lead extended), and cut it out using a utility knife.

4. Remove the template, and fold along the scored line. Apply glue to the paste overlaps to hold the paper together.

5. Temporarily attach the door mechanism template to the leftover paper. Score the fold lines by tracing them with the tip of a mechanical pencil (without any lead extended), and cut out the door mechanism using a utility knife. Remove the template.

6. Insert the pull-tab mechanism into the slit in the card base.

7. Paste the door mechanism to the pull-tab mechanism, sandwiching it around the tab's narrowed tip.

8. Turn the card over. Fold the pull-tab mechanism along the scored lines.

9. Turn the card over again to the front, and using paste attach the color photocopies of the plate with fishbone and the cat.

10. Flip over the door mechanism, and using paste attach the color photocopy of the plate with fish and the cat.

11. Write your message using rubber stamps, and pull on the tab mechanism, adjusting as needed. Apply glue to the interior of the card base, and attach together.

SHEEPHERDING DOG

The dog is chasing a little lamb. Or so it seems . . . until you pull the tab and, one after

another, out come the big sheep! Use this card for all sorts of ideas.

Instructions on page 124

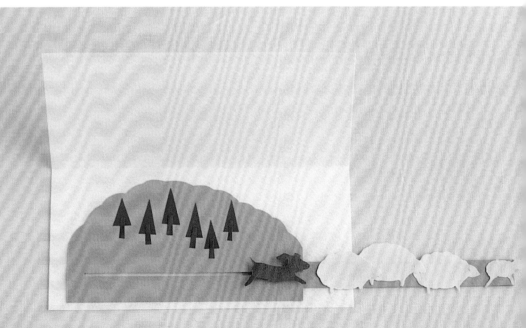

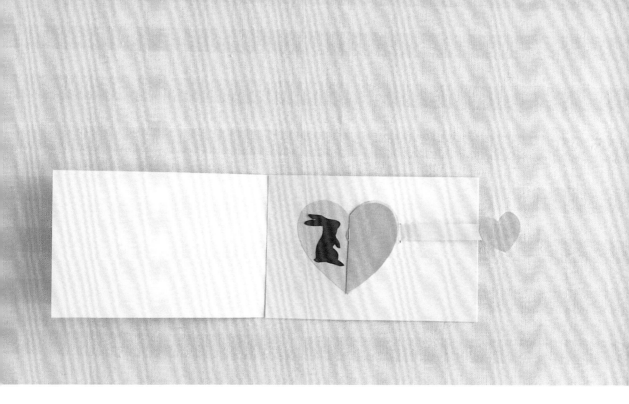

LOVE BUNNY

This bunny delivers a love note. Pull the heart tab to reveal a confession of "I love you."

What a fun way to express such a wonderful sentiment!

Instructions on pages 126 and 127

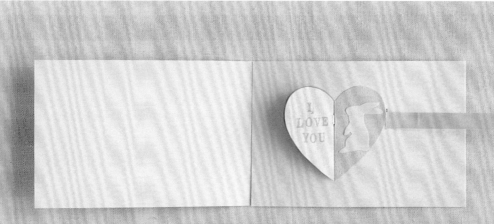

Amazing Card 3

CARDS THAT SPIN

Cut out a circle, and fasten the middle inside the card base so that the circle moves. You'll have so much fun creating different designs that shift as you spin them around, you'll be hooked!

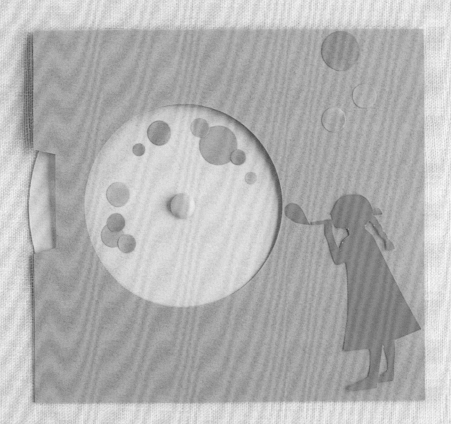

SOAP BUBBLES

The girl looks as if she's enjoying herself, blowing soap bubbles as they spin around. This card becomes a toy for whoever receives it. Anyone would want to spin and play with it over and over again. Spread out the soap bubbles for a balanced effect.

MATERIALS

1 sheet of 8½" × 11" (21.5 cm × 28 cm) Canson Mi-Teintes paper for the card base

1 sheet of 8½" × 11" (21.5 cm × 28 cm) Canson Mi-Teintes paper for the circle

1 split pin

Color photocopies of the card motifs (girl and soap bubbles, page 141)

1. Fold the card base in half, and cut it to card size using a utility knife with the fold on the top. (The unfolded card base will be 4¼" × 8" [11 cm x 20 cm].)

2. With the card open, temporarily attach the circle template using masking tape, and cut a circle with a radius of 1⅛" (2.7 cm) using a circle cutter. Remove the template. Mark the center of the circle using a mechanical pencil.

3. Temporarily attach the circle template to Mi-Teintes paper, and cut a circle with a radius of 1¾" (4.3 cm) using a circle cutter. Remove the template. Mark the center of the circle using a mechanical pencil.

4. Place the circle inside the card base, and align the circles' centers. Make a hole in the center using an awl.

5. Insert the split pin, fastening it from the other side.

6. With the card open, attach the color photocopies of the soap bubbles using paste.

7. With the card closed, attach the color photocopy of the girl and more soap bubbles using paste.

8. Apply glue inside the card along its right side, and, closing the card, attach it together.

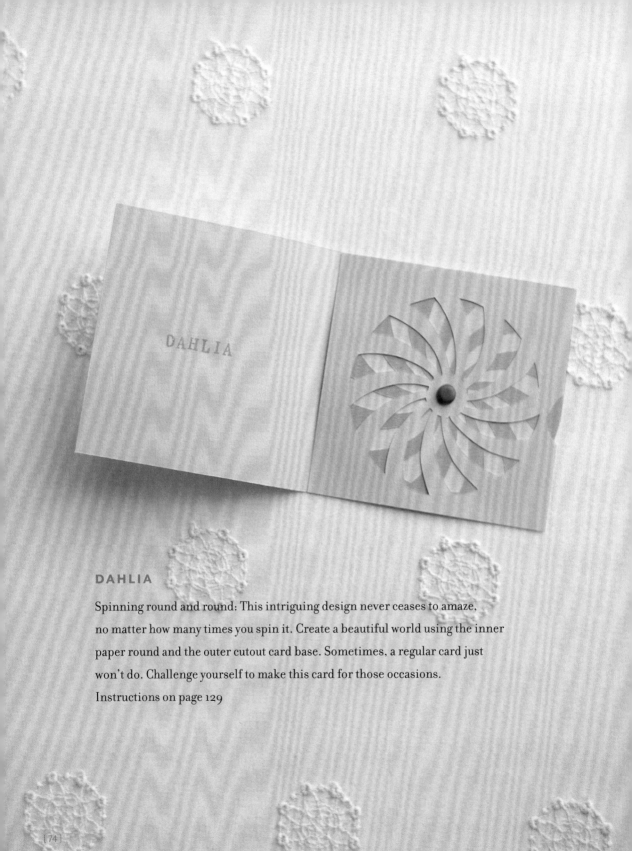

DAHLIA

DAHLIA

Spinning round and round: This intriguing design never ceases to amaze, no matter how many times you spin it. Create a beautiful world using the inner paper round and the outer cutout card base. Sometimes, a regular card just won't do. Challenge yourself to make this card for those occasions.

Instructions on page 129

CIRCUS ELEPHANT

The elephant appears to balance atop the ball as it spins around. Make the interior paper circle with two colors to heighten the spinning effect. Looks like a fun circus!

Instructions on pages 130 and 131

Amazing Card 4

CARDS THAT SPRING

These cards offer a high level of surprise, with their hidden motifs that pop up when you open them. Their charm has the power to take you back to your childhood.

HOPPING BUNNY

Open the card, and the bunny springs playfully out of a thicket! The simple mountain-and-valley fold construction is part of this card's appeal. It needs strength to bounce, so thick paper is recommended.

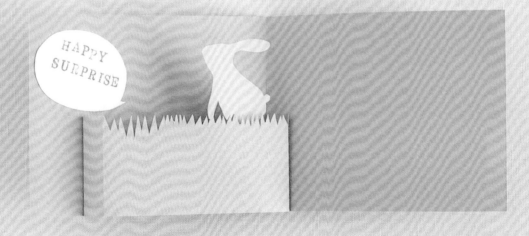

MATERIALS

1 sheet of 8½" × 11" (21.5 cm × 28 cm) card stock for the card base and thicket

¼ sheet of 8½" × 11" (21.5 cm × 28 cm) Canson Mi-Teintes paper for the bunny

Color photocopy of motif (message, page 142)

1. Cut the card base to card size using a utility knife.

2. Temporarily attach the template to the card base using masking tape, and trace the paste overlap with the tip of a mechanical pencil (without any lead extended). Remove the template.

3. Temporarily attach the thicket template to the leftover paper. Score the fold lines by tracing them with the tip of a mechanical pencil (without any lead extended), and cut out using scissors. Remove the template.

4. Temporarily attach the bunny template to the Mi-Teintes paper. Score the fold lines by tracing them with the tip of a mechanical pencil (without any lead extended), and cut out using scissors. Remove the template.

5. Turn over the thicket paper, and glue it to the card base on the traced paste overlap.

6. Turn the bunny cutout over, and paste it on top of the thicket.

7. Fold the bunny along the scored lines, and paste down the other side.

8. Fold the thicket along the scored lines, and paste down the other side. Attach the color photocopy of the message using paste.

MAGIC SHOW

When you open this card, a white dove pops out of the silk top hat. It's as much fun as watching a real magic show! You can also challenge yourself to use this technique for charming a snake out of a pot.

Instructions on pages 133 and 134

BIRTHDAY WISHES

This "card within a card" is truly original. When the message you want to convey appears inside, it has tremendous impact. Have fun making different birthday cards featuring a cake, or whatever you like, that pops out.

Instructions on pages 135 and 136

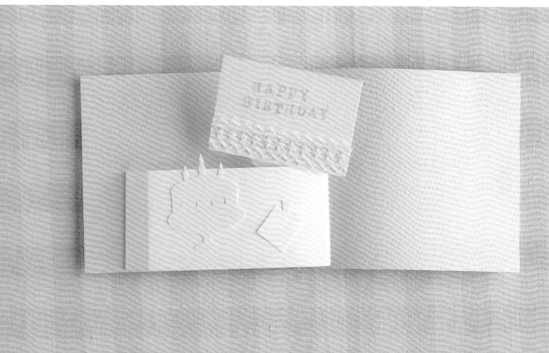

My Favorite Pop-up Book

People often ask me, "I want to give a book to my friend's child; do you have any suggestions?" I always recommend this book: *One Red Dot* by David A. Carter. Each two-page spread is a pop-up that incorporates simple shapes and colors and features a hide-and-seek with one red dot. The spectacular combinations are utterly charming. The book is not only for children—I also recommend it for adults. I've looked at it dozens of times myself, yet each time I open this book, the pop-ups never fail to delight and surprise me with new discoveries. I often take a break from work with a cup of tea or relax before bed by spending a little time with my favorite pop-up book.

How to Make the Cards

All the templates are full size. You may choose to either photocopy or trace them.

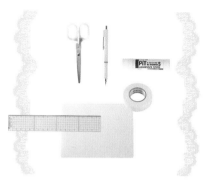

Tools

Scissors, mechanical pencil, glue, utility knife, ruler, masking tape, cutting mat

Gift Box

Photograph on page 12

Instructions on page 13

Size: 3½" × 6¼" (9 cm × 16 cm)

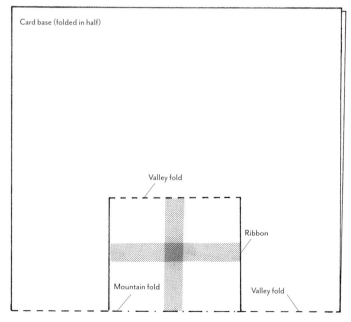

Card base (folded in half)

Valley fold

Ribbon

Mountain fold

Valley fold

Strawberry and Pear

Photograph on page 14

Size: 2¾" × 4¾" (7 cm × 12 cm)

MATERIALS FOR STRAWBERRY (LEFT)

1 sheet of 8½" × 11" (21.5 cm × 28 cm) Canson Mi-Teintes paper for the card base

1 piece of fabric 1¼" × 1¼" (3 cm × 3 cm) for the strawberry

1 piece of fabric ⅞" × ⅞" (2 cm × 2 cm) for the strawberry top

MATERIALS FOR PEAR (RIGHT)

1 sheet of 8½" × 11" (21.5 cm × 28 cm) Canson Mi-Teintes paper for the card base

1 piece of fabric 1¼" × 1¼" (3 cm × 3 cm) for the pear

1 piece of fabric ⅜" × ⅞" (1 cm × 2 cm) for the leaf

1 piece of wire ⅜" (1 cm) long

INSTRUCTIONS

1. Cut each card base to the card size (two pieces, interior and exterior) using a utility knife.

2. Temporarily attach the template to the interior piece using masking tape, and cut the design through the template.

3. Score the fold lines by tracing them with the tip of a mechanical pencil (without any lead extended).

4. Remove the template, and fold along the scored lines. Keeping the card closed, crease the folds.

5. For the strawberry card, paste on the fabric cut in a strawberry shape. Paste the fabric cut in a stem shape above. For the pear card, take the two pieces of fabric cut in the leaf shape, and paste them together around the wire. Paste the end of the wire to the paper. Paste the fabric cut in the pear shape on top of it.

6. Write your message using rubber stamps.

7. Paste the exterior piece to the back of the interior piece.

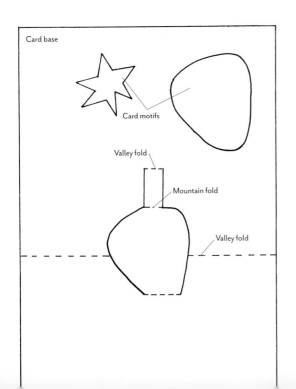

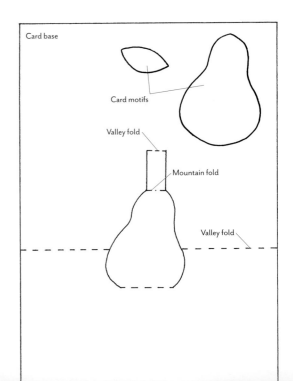

Ballerina Dancing Onstage

Photograph on page 15

Template on page 84

Card motif on page 137

Size: 4" × 7⅛" (10 cm × 18 cm)

MATERIALS

1 sheet of 8½" × 11" (21.5 cm × 28 cm) card stock for the card base

1 piece of ⅜" (0.9 cm) wide lace ribbon 2¾" (7 cm) long

Color photocopy of card motif (ballerina)

INSTRUCTIONS

1. Cut each card base to card size (two pieces, interior and exterior) using a utility knife.

2. Temporarily attach the template to the interior piece using masking tape, and cut the design through the template.

3. Score the fold lines by tracing them with the tip of a mechanical pencil (without any lead extended).

4. Remove the template, and fold along the scored lines. Keeping the card closed, crease the folds.

5. Paste the exterior piece to the back of the interior piece.

6. Attach the color photocopy of the ballerina using paste.

7. Attach the lace ribbon using adhesive.

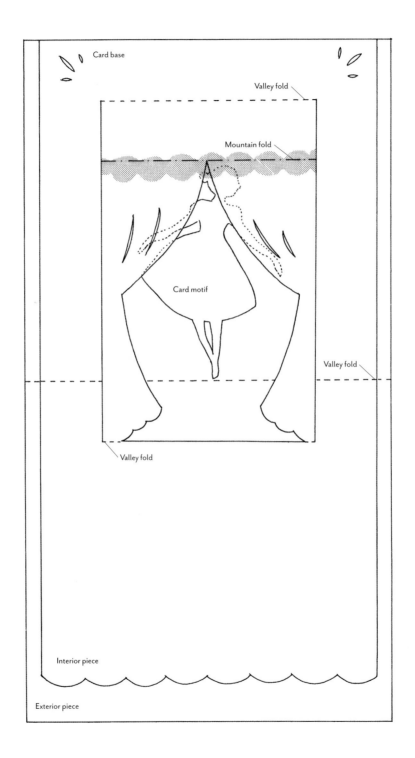

Card base

Valley fold

Mountain fold

Card motif

Valley fold

Valley fold

Interior piece

Exterior piece

Card base (folded in half)

Valley fold

Mountain fold

Mountain fold

Valley fold

Hula Girls

Photograph on page 16

Instructions on page 17

Size: 7½" × 3⅛" (19.5 cm × 8 cm)

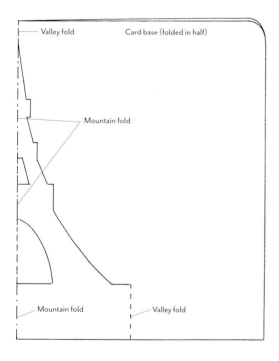

Valley fold   Card base (folded in half)

Mountain fold

Mountain fold   Valley fold

Parisian Scene

Photograph on page 18

Card motif on page 137

Size: 5⅜" × 3¼" (13.5 cm × 8.5 cm)

MATERIALS

1 sheet of 8½" × 11" (21.5 cm × 28 cm) Canson Mi-Teintes paper for the card base

1 sheet of wrapping paper 5⅜" × 3¼" (13.5 cm × 8.5 cm)

1 ticket stub from a trip

Color photocopy of card motif (girl)

INSTRUCTIONS

1. Cut the card base to card size (two pieces, interior and exterior) using a utility knife. Cut the wrapping paper to the same size.

2. Temporarily attach the template to the interior piece using masking tape, and cut the design through the template.

3. Score the fold lines by tracing with the tip of a mechanical pencil (without any lead extended).

4. Remove the template, and fold along the scored lines. Keeping the card closed, crease the folds.

5. Attach the ticket and the color photocopy of the girl using paste.

6. Attach the wrapping paper and the exterior piece to the back of the interior piece using paste.

Ribbon

Photograph on page 19

Size: 5¾" × 2¾" (12 cm × 7 cm)

MATERIALS

1 sheet of 8½" × 11" (21.5 cm × 28 cm) Canson Mi-Teintes paper for the card base

INSTRUCTIONS

1. Cut the card base to card size (two pieces, interior and exterior) using a utility knife.

2. Temporarily attach the template to the interior piece using masking tape, and cut the design through the template.

3. Score the fold lines by tracing with the tip of a mechanical pencil (without any lead extended).

4. Remove the template, and fold along the scored lines. Keeping the card closed, crease the folds.

5. Write your message using rubber stamps.

6. Attach the exterior piece to the back of the interior piece using paste.

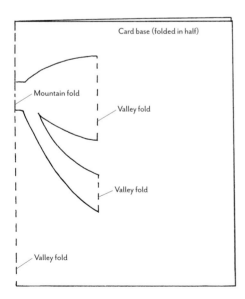

Raindrops

Photograph on page 20

Instructions on page 21

Card motifs on page 137

Size: 5½" × 6" (14 cm × 15 cm)

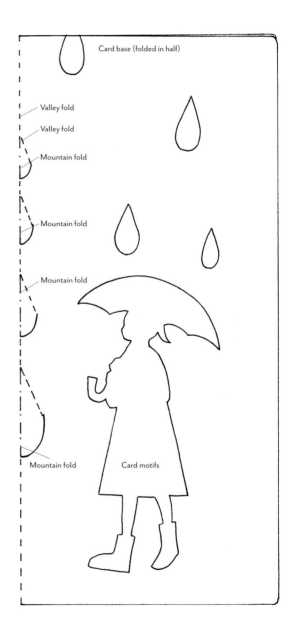

Teatime

Photograph on page 22

Card motif on page 137

Size: 5½" × 3¾" (13.5 cm × 7 cm)

MATERIALS

1 sheet of 8½" × 11" (21.5 cm × 28 cm) card stock for the interior card base

1 sheet of 8½" × 11" (21.5 cm × 28 cm) Canson Mi-Teintes paper for the exterior card base

1 piece of fabric 2⅜" × 2⅜" (6 cm × 6 cm)

1 piece of ⅜" (0.8 cm) wide lace ribbon 3½" (9 cm) long

Color photocopy of the card motif (steam)

INSTRUCTIONS

1. Cut the card base and Mi-Teintes paper to card size.

2. Temporarily attach the template to the interior piece using masking tape, and cut the design through the template.

3. Score the fold lines by tracing with the tip of a mechanical pencil (without any lead extended).

4. Remove the template, and fold along scored lines. Keeping the card closed, crease the folds.

5. Cut a teapot and tea cup shape out of the fabric, and glue them to the interior piece along with the lace ribbon and the color photocopy of steam.

6. Paste the exterior piece to the back of the interior piece.

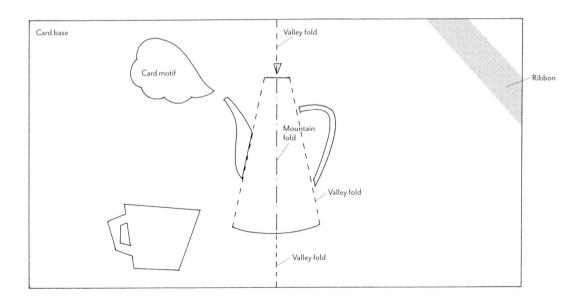

Three Sisters

Photograph on page 23

Card motif on page 137

Size: 3½" × 3½" (9 cm × 9 cm)

MATERIALS

3 sheets of 8½" × 11" (21.5 cm × 28 cm) scrapbooking paper for the card base

Ribbon, as needed

Color photocopies of card motifs (girls)

INSTRUCTIONS

1. Cut each card base to card size.

2. Temporarily attach the template to the card base using masking tape, and cut the design through the template.

3. Score the fold lines, tracing with the tip of a mechanical pencil (without any lead extended).

4. Remove the template, and fold along scored lines. Keeping the card closed, crease the folds.

5. Attach each color photocopy of girl using paste.

6. Attach ribbon to the girls' waists using adhesive.

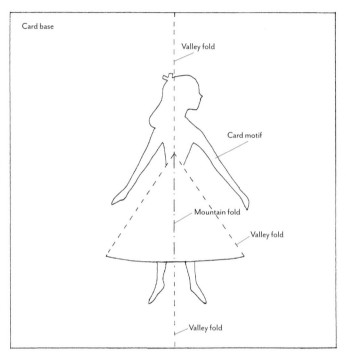

Spring's Arrival

Photograph on page 24

Instructions on page 25

Card motifs on page 138

Size: 10¼" × 2⅜" (26 cm × 6 cm)

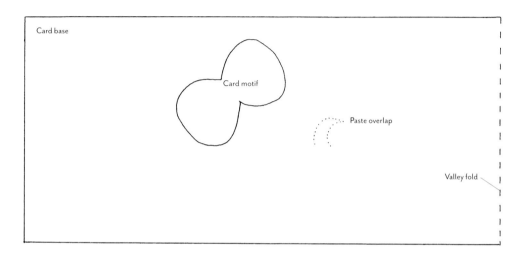

Card base

Card motif

Paste overlap

Valley fold

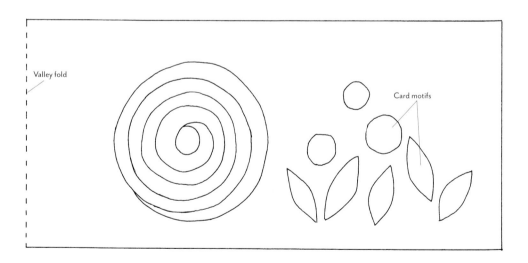

Valley fold

Card motifs

Sweethearts

Photograph on page 26

Card motifs on page 138

Size: 8½" × 3¼" (21.5 cm × 8.5 cm)

MATERIALS

1 sheet of 8½" × 11" (21.5 cm × 28 cm) card stock for the card base

1 sheet of 8½" × 11" (21.5 cm × 28 cm) Canson Mi-Teintes paper for the coil

Color photocopies of card motifs (boy and girl)

INSTRUCTIONS

1. Cut the card base to card size.

2. Temporarily attach the template to the card base using masking tape, and trace the position of the end of the coil with the tip of a mechanical pencil (without any lead extended).

3. Temporarily attach the coil template to the Mi-Teintes paper, and cut out the design. Remove the template.

4. Apply glue to tip of the coil, and attach the coil at the position traced on the card base.

5. Apply glue to the other tip of the coil in the center; close the card, and press down to attach the coil.

6. Open the card, and attach the color photocopies of the boy and girl using paste.

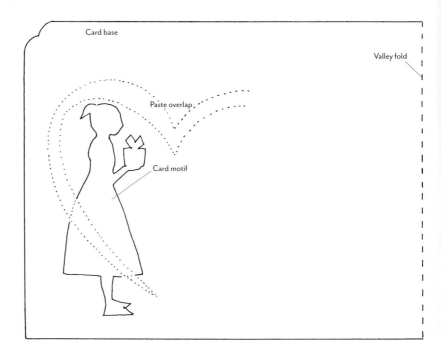

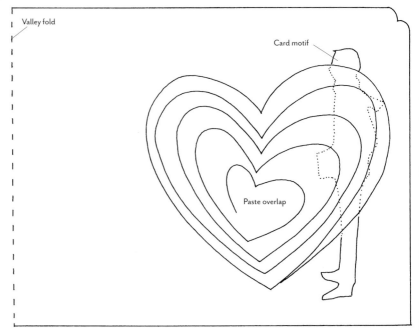

The North Wind and the Sun

Photograph on page 27

Card motifs on page 138

Size: 11½" × 4¼" (29 cm × 11 cm)

MATERIALS

1 sheet of 8½" × 11" (21.5 cm × 28 cm) card stock for the card base

1 sheet of 8½" × 11" (21.5 cm × 28 cm) Canson Mi-Teintes paper for the coil

Color photocopies of card motifs (sun, cloud, fallen leaves, traveler)

INSTRUCTIONS

1. Cut the card base to card size.

2. Temporarily attach the template to the card base using masking tape, and trace the position of the end of the coil with the tip of a mechanical pencil (without any lead extended).

3. Temporarily attach the coil template to the Mi-Teintes paper, and cut out the design. Remove the template.

4. Apply glue to the tip of the coil, and attach the coil at the position traced on the card base.

5. Apply glue to the other tip of coil in the center; close the card, and press down to attach the coil.

6. Open the card, and attach the color photocopies of the sun, cloud, fallen leaves, and traveler using paste.

Card base

Card motifs

Paste overlap

Card motif

Valley fold

TEMPLATE CONTINUES ON NEXT PAGE

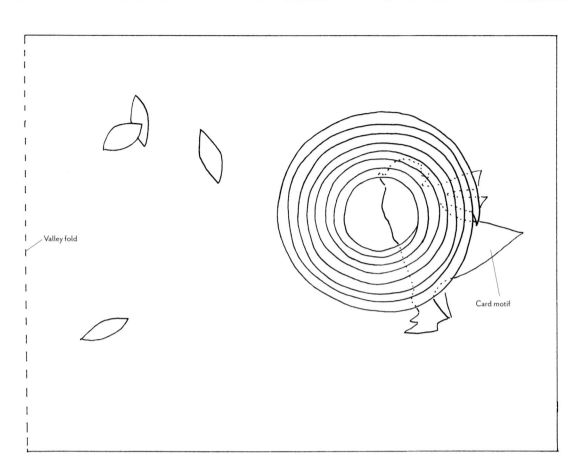

Valley fold

Card motif

Pierrot Hat

Photograph on page 28

Instructions on page 29

Size: 6⅝" × 2⅝" (6.5 cm × 17 cm)

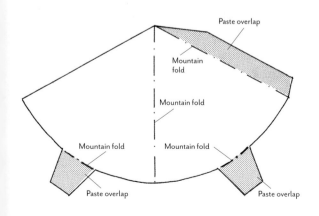

Paste overlap

Mountain fold

Mountain fold

Mountain fold

Mountain fold

Paste overlap

Paste overlap

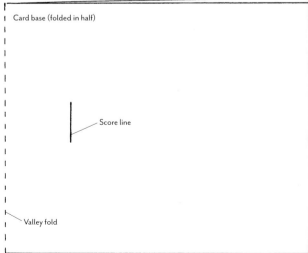

Card base (folded in half)

Score line

Valley fold

Happy Halloween

Photograph on page 30

Card motif on page 138

Size: 7" × 4" (18 cm × 10 cm)

MATERIALS

1 sheet of 8½" × 11" (21.5 cm × 28 cm) Canson Mi-Teintes paper for the card base

1 sheet of 8½" × 11" (21.5 cm × 28 cm) Canson Mi-Teintes paper for the hat

Pipe cleaner, as needed

Color photocopy of the card motif (pumpkin)

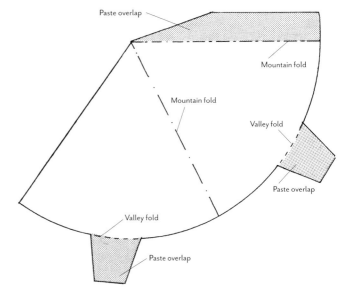

INSTRUCTIONS

1. Cut the card base to card size.

2. Cut a circle 2⅝" (6.5 cm) in diameter out of the Mi-Teintes paper, and paste it to the center of the card base.

3. Temporarily attach the template to the card base using masking tape, and cut slits through the template. Remove the template.

4. Temporarily attach the cone template to the leftover Mi-Teintes paper, and cut out the design.

5. Score the fold lines by tracing with the tip of a mechanical pencil (without any lead extended).

6. Remove the template, apply glue to the paste overlap, and connect the cone.

7. Insert the tabs into the slits in the card base, apply glue to the underside of the tabs, and paste them to the surface of the card.

8. Paste the pipe cleaner to the color photocopy of a pumpkin, attach the pumpkin to the hat, and write your message using rubber stamps.

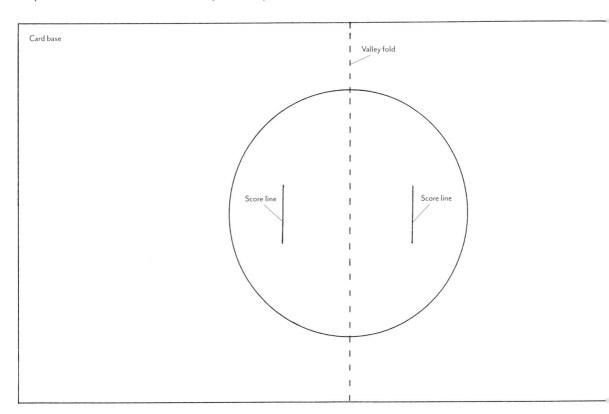

Woodland Friends

Photograph on page 31

Card motifs on page 138

Size: 6¼" × 4⅜" (16 cm × 11 cm)

MATERIALS

1 sheet of 8½" × 11"
(21.5 cm × 28 cm) card
stock for card base

1 sheet of 8½" × 11"
(21.5 cm × 28 cm)
Canson Mi-Teintes paper
for the trees

Color photocopy of
card motifs (bird,
squirrel, rabbit, fawn)

INSTRUCTIONS

1. Cut the card base to card size.

2. Temporarily attach the template to the
card base using masking tape, and cut slits
through the template. Remove the template.

3. Temporarily attach the cone template to
the Mi-Teintes paper, and cut out the design.

4. Score the fold lines by tracing with the
tip of a mechanical pencil (without any
lead extended).

5. Remove the template, apply glue to the
paste overlap, and connect the cone.

6. Insert tabs into the slits of the card base,
apply glue to the underside of the tabs, and
paste them to the surface of the card.

7. Attach color photocopies of the bird,
squirrel, rabbit, and fawn using paste.

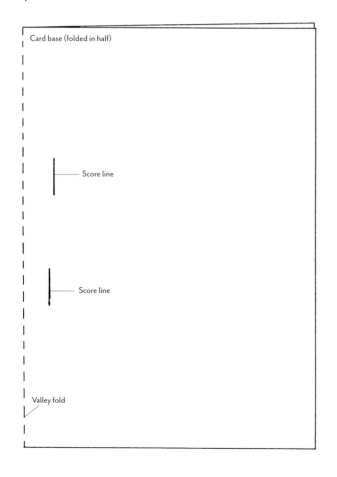

Card base (folded in half)

Score line

Score line

Valley fold

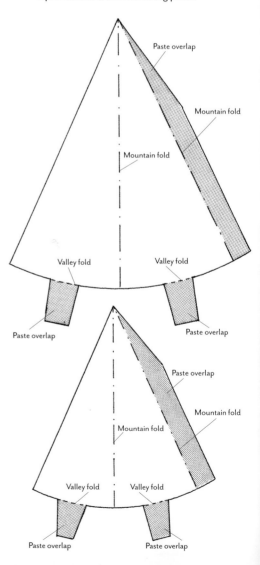

Paste overlap

Mountain fold

Mountain fold

Valley fold

Valley fold

Paste overlap

Paste overlap

Paste overlap

Mountain fold

Mountain fold

Valley fold

Valley fold

Paste overlap

Paste overlap

Strawberry Basket

Photograph on page 32

Instructions on page 33

Card motifs on page 139

Size: 6¼" × 4" (16 cm × 10 cm)

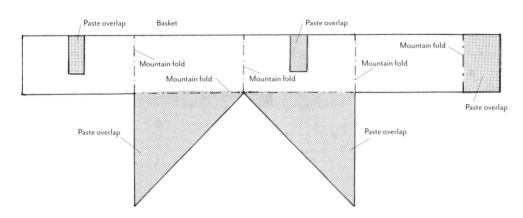

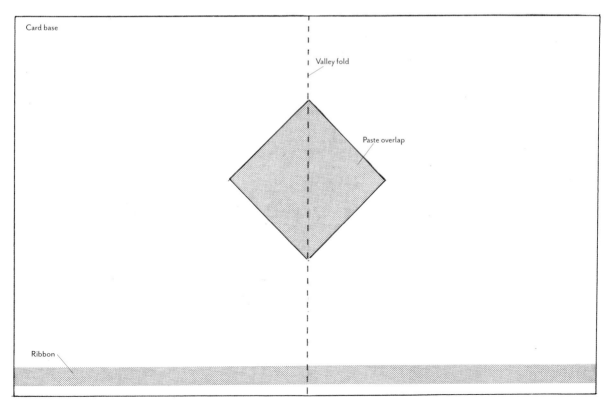

Rabbit in the Briar

Photograph on page 34

Card motifs on page 139

Size: 6¼" × 3½" (16 cm × 9 cm)

MATERIALS

1 sheet of 8½" × 11" (21.5 cm × 28 cm) card stock for the card base

1 sheet of 8½" × 11" (21.5 cm × 28 cm) Canson Mi-Teintes paper for the briar

Color photocopy of the card motif (rabbit)

INSTRUCTIONS

1. Cut the card base to card size.

2. Temporarily attach the template to the card base using masking tape, and trace the position where the briar will be attached (the paste overlap) using the tip of a mechanical pencil (without any lead extended). Remove the template.

3. Temporarily attach the briar template to the Mi-Teintes paper, and score fold lines by tracing with the tip of a mechanical pencil (without any lead extended).

4. Cut out the briar, remove the template, and fold along the scored lines. Apply glue to the paste overlap, and connect the briar.

5. Apply glue to one of the briar's triangular paste overlaps, and attach it at the position traced on the card base. Apply glue to the other triangular paste overlap, and close the card to secure it.

6. Attach the color photocopy of the rabbit using paste.

7. Write your message using rubber stamps.

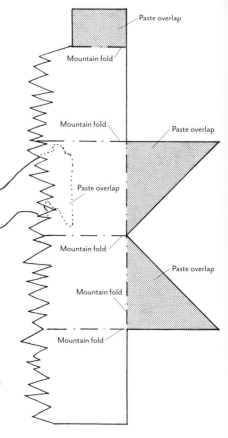

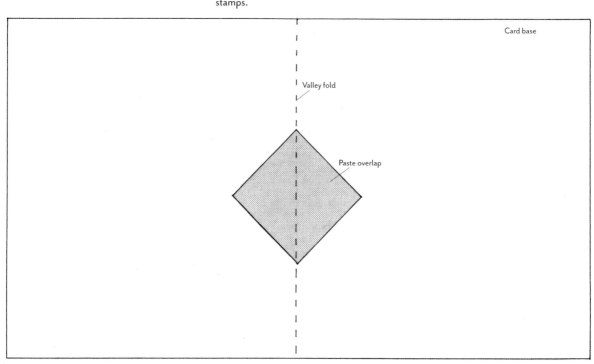

My House

Photograph on page 35

Size: 3½" × 6¼" (16 cm × 9 cm)

MATERIALS

1 sheet of 8½" × 11" (21.5 cm × 28 cm) card stock for the card base

2 pieces of fabric 1½" × 1½" each (4 cm × 4 cm)

INSTRUCTIONS

1. Cut the card base to card size.

2. Temporarily attach the template to the card base using masking tape, and trace the position where house will be attached using the tip of a mechanical pencil (without any lead extended). Remove the template.

3. Temporarily attach the house template to the leftover paper, and score the fold lines by tracing them with the tip of a mechanical pencil (without any lead extended).

4. Cut out the house and windows.

5. Remove the template, fold along scored lines, and attach the fabric cut in roof shapes using adhesive. Apply glue to the paste overlap, and connect the house.

6. Apply glue to one of the house's triangular paste overlaps, and attach it at the position traced on the card base. Apply glue to the other triangular paste overlap, and close the card to secure it.

7. Write your message using rubber stamps.

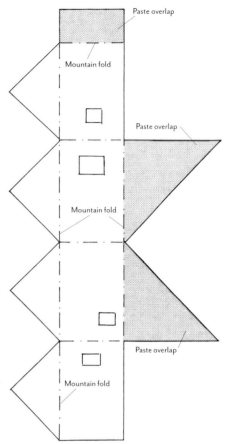

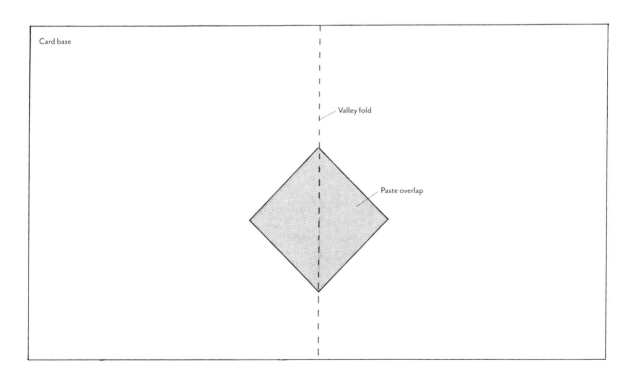

Special Delivery Present

Photograph
on page 40

Card motifs
on page 139

Size: 3¾" × 8½"
(9.5 cm × 22 cm)

MATERIALS

1 sheet of 8½" × 11" (21.5 cm × 28 cm)
card stock for the card base

1 sheet of 8½" × 11" (21.5 cm × 28 cm)
Canson Mi-Teintes paper for the coil

1 piece of ½" (1.5 cm) wide lace ribbon
5" (13 cm) long

Color photocopies of card motifs
(gift box, ribbon, bird)

INSTRUCTIONS

1. Cut the card base to card size.

2. Temporarily attach the template to
the card base using masking tape, and
trace the position of the end of the
coil with the tip of a mechanical pencil
(without any lead extended).

3. Temporarily attach the coil template
to the Mi-Teintes paper, and cut out the
design. Remove the template.

4. Attach a color photocopy of the bird
using paste; apply glue to the tip of the
coil, and attach at the position traced on
the card base.

5. Apply glue to the center of the other
tip of the coil; close the card, and press
down to attach the coil.

6. Open the card, and attach color
photocopies of the gift box and ribbon
using paste.

7. Attach the lace ribbon using adhesive,
and write your message using rubber
stamps.

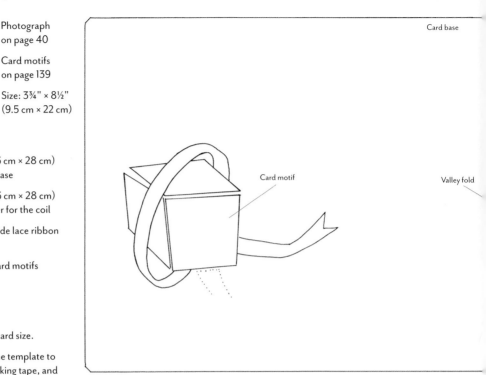

Card base

Card motif

Valley fold

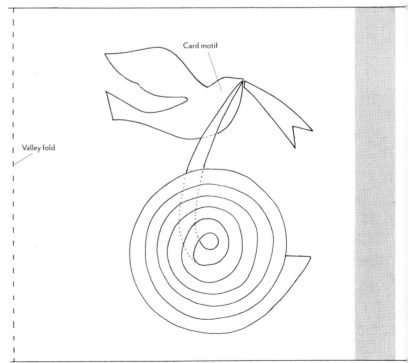

Card motif

Valley fold

Birthday Cake

Photograph on page 41

Card motif on page 139

Size: 7" × 6¼" (18 cm × 16 cm)

MATERIALS

1 sheet of 8½" × 11" (21.5 cm × 28 cm)
Canson Mi-Teintes paper for the card base

1 piece of metallic string 2¾" (7 cm) long

1 piece of very thin lace ribbon 23½" (60 cm) long

Color photocopy of card motif (cake)

INSTRUCTIONS

1. Cut the card base to card size (two pieces, interior and exterior) using a utility knife.

2. Temporarily attach the template to the interior piece using masking tape, and cut the design through the template.

3. Score the fold lines by tracing them with the tip of a mechanical pencil (without any lead extended).

4. Turn the card over, and score the fold lines in the same way.

5. Remove the template, and fold along the scored lines. Keeping the card closed, crease the folds.

6. Attach the color photocopy of the cake using paste.

7. Paste the metallic string to the cake. Write your message using rubber stamps, and make dots with a cotton swab.

8. Attach the lace ribbon to the front of the exterior sheet using adhesive.

9. Paste the front of the exterior sheet to the back of the interior piece.

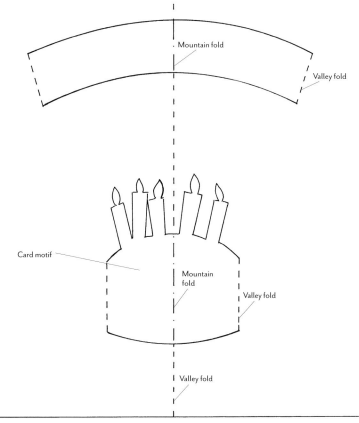

Card base

Bouquet

Photograph on page 41

Card motif on page 139

Size: 4¾" × 4¾" (12 cm × 12 cm)

MATERIALS

1 sheet of 8½" × 11" (21.5 cm × 28 cm) card stock for the card base

1 piece of thin lace ribbon 4" (10 cm) long

Color photocopy of the card motif (flowers)

INSTRUCTIONS

1. Cut the card base to card size.

2. Temporarily attach the template to the card base using masking tape, and cut the design through the template.

3. Score the fold lines by tracing with the tip of a mechanical pencil (without any lead extended).

4. Remove the template, and fold along the scored lines. Keeping the card closed, crease the folds.

5. Attach the color photocopy of the flowers using paste.

6. Tie the ribbon in a bow, and attach the bow using adhesive.

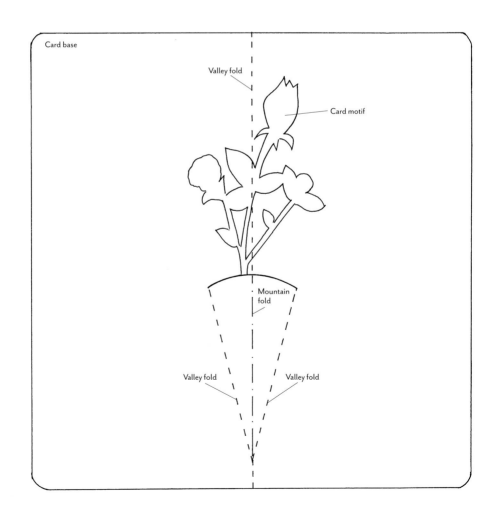

Crown

Photograph on page 42

Size: 4¾" × 3¾" (12 cm × 9.5 cm)

MATERIALS

1 sheet of 8½" × 11" (21.5 cm × 28 cm) Canson Mi-Teintes paper for the card base

1 sheet of 8½" × 11" (21.5 cm × 28 cm) heavy paper for the crown

1 piece of metallic ribbon 6" (15 cm) long

6 beads 3 mm in diameter

INSTRUCTIONS

1. Cut the card base to card size.

2. Temporarily attach the template to the card base using masking tape, and cut slits through the template. Remove the template.

3. Temporarily attach the cone template to the heavy paper, and cut out the design.

4. Score fold lines by tracing with the tip of a mechanical pencil (without any lead extended).

5. Remove the template, apply glue to the paste overlap, and connect the cone.

6. Insert tabs into the slits in the card base, apply glue to underside of the tabs, and attach them to the surface of the card.

7. Attach the metallic ribbon and beads using adhesive.

8. Write your message using rubber stamps.

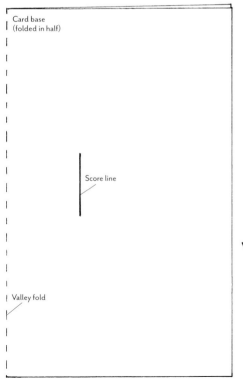

Card base
(folded in half)

Score line

Valley fold

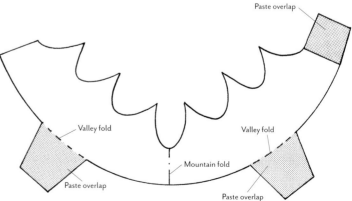

Paste overlap

Valley fold

Valley fold

Mountain fold

Paste overlap

Paste overlap

Chic Bunny

Photograph on page 43

Size: 3⅛" × 6½" (8 cm × 16.5 cm)

MATERIALS

1 sheet of 8½" × 11" (21.5 cm × 28 cm) card stock for the card base

1 sheet of 8½" × 11" (21.5 cm × 28 cm) scrapbooking paper for the interior

1 piece of very thin ribbon 3⅛" (8 cm) long

INSTRUCTIONS

1. Cut the card base to card size.

2. Temporarily attach the template to the interior piece using masking tape, and cut the design through the template.

3. Score the fold lines by tracing them with the tip of a mechanical pencil (without any lead extended).

4. Remove the template, and fold along the scored lines. Keeping the card closed, crease the folds.

5. Attach the ribbon using adhesive.

6. Write your message using rubber stamps.

7. Paste the card base to the back of the interior piece.

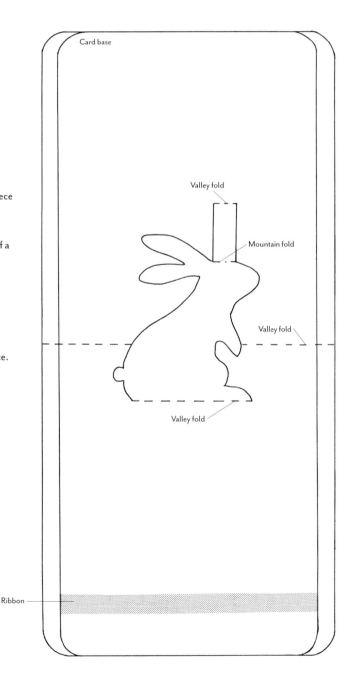

Card base

Valley fold

Mountain fold

Valley fold

Valley fold

Ribbon

Birthday Party

Photograph on page 44

Size: 7½" × 5½" (14 cm × 19 cm)

MATERIALS

1 sheet of 8½" × 11" (21.5 cm × 28 cm) scrapbooking paper for the card base

1 sheet of 8½" × 11" (21.5 cm × 28 cm) Canson Mi-Teintes paper for the interior piece

1 piece of ½" (1.5 cm) wide lace ribbon 3⅜" (8.5 cm) long

INSTRUCTIONS

1. Cut the card base to card size.

2. Temporarily attach the template to the Mi-Teintes paper using masking tape, and cut design through the template.

3. Score the fold lines by tracing with the tip of a mechanical pencil (without any lead extended).

4. Remove the template, and fold along the scored lines. Keeping the card closed, crease the folds.

5. Paste the interior piece to the card base.

6. Attach lace ribbon using an adhesive, and write your message using rubber stamps.

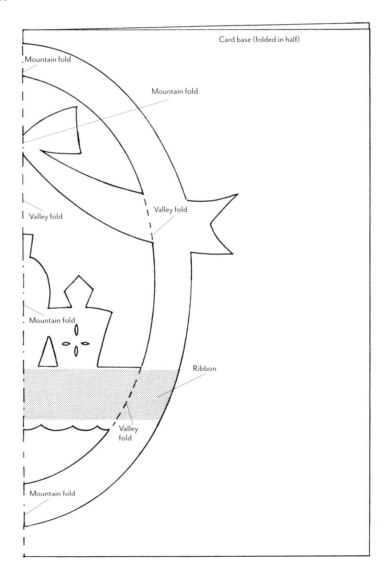

Card base (folded in half)

Mountain fold

Mountain fold

Valley fold

Valley fold

Mountain fold

Ribbon

Valley fold

Mountain fold

Birthday Gifts

Photograph on page 45

Size: 5⅛" × 4⅜" (13 cm × 11 cm)

MATERIALS

1 sheet of 8½" × 11" (21.5 cm × 28 cm) card stock for the card base

1 piece of fabric ¾" × ½" (2 cm × 1.5 cm) for the gift on the left

1 piece of fabric 1½" × 1⅛" (4 cm × 3 cm) for the gift in the center

1 piece of fabric 1⅛" × ½" (3 cm × 1.5 cm) for the gift on the right

1 piece of very thin ribbon 2" (5 cm) long for the gift on the left

1 piece of very thin ribbon 6" (15 cm) long for the gift in the center

1 piece of ⅛" (0.5 cm) wide rickrack 1⅛" (3 cm) long for the gift on the right

INSTRUCTIONS

1. Cut the card base to card size.

2. Temporarily attach the template to the card base using masking tape, and cut the design through the template.

3. Score the fold lines by tracing with the tip of a mechanical pencil (without any lead extended).

4. Remove the template, and fold along the scored lines. Keeping the card closed, crease the folds.

5. Paste fabric on each gift then paste ribbon in position. Tie a decorative bow, and attach the bow on top.

6. Write your message using rubber stamps.

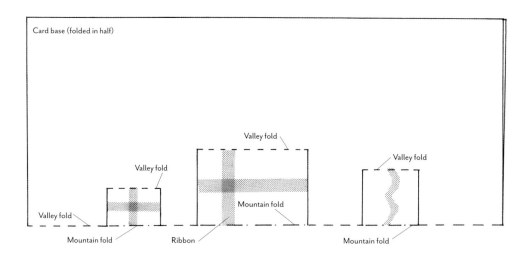

Festive Village

Photograph on page 48

Size: 10¼" × 4" (10 cm × 26 cm)

MATERIALS

1 sheet of 8½" × 11" (21.5 cm × 28 cm) watercolor paper for the card base interior

1 sheet of 8½" × 11" (21.5 cm × 28 cm) watercolor paper for the card base exterior

INSTRUCTIONS

1. Cut each card base to card size (two pieces, interior and exterior) using a utility knife.

2. Temporarily attach the template to the interior piece using masking tape, and cut the design through the template.

3. Score the fold lines by tracing with the tip of a mechanical pencil (without any lead extended).

4. Remove the template, and fold along the scored lines. Keeping the card closed, crease the folds.

5. Make falling snow using a cotton swab dipped in ink.

6. Paste the exterior card base to the back of the interior piece.

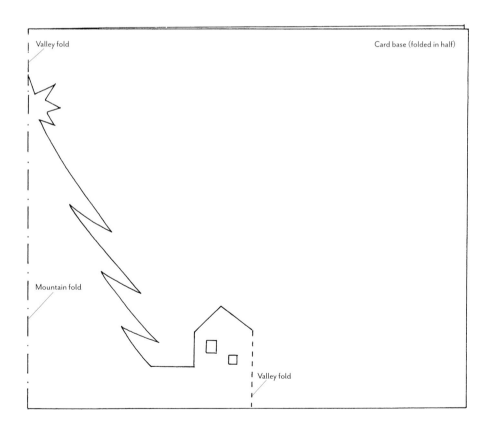

Valley fold

Card base (folded in half)

Mountain fold

Valley fold

Wintry Mountain Deer

Photograph on page 49

Card motifs on page 139

Size: 10¼" × 4" (26 cm × 10 cm)

MATERIALS

1 sheet of 8½" × 11" (21.5 cm × 28 cm) card stock for the card base

1 sheet of 8½" × 11" (21.5 cm × 28 cm) Canson Mi-Teintes paper for the tree

Color photocopies of the card

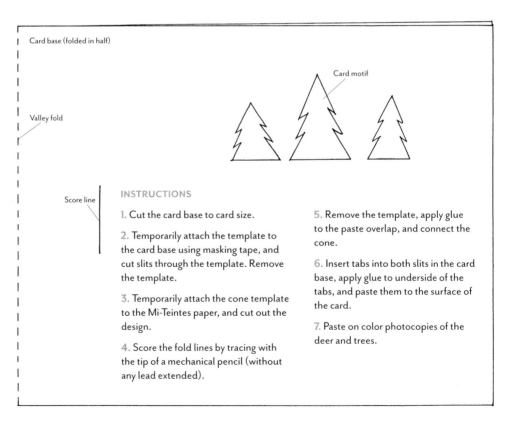

Paste overlap

Mountain fold

Mountain fold

Paste overlap   Valley fold   Valley fold   Paste overlap

Card base (folded in half)

Valley fold

Card motif

Score line

INSTRUCTIONS

1. Cut the card base to card size.

2. Temporarily attach the template to the card base using masking tape, and cut slits through the template. Remove the template.

3. Temporarily attach the cone template to the Mi-Teintes paper, and cut out the design.

4. Score the fold lines by tracing with the tip of a mechanical pencil (without any lead extended).

5. Remove the template, apply glue to the paste overlap, and connect the cone.

6. Insert tabs into both slits in the card base, apply glue to underside of the tabs, and paste them to the surface of the card.

7. Paste on color photocopies of the deer and trees.

Stocking and Snowman

Photograph on page 50

Size: 2¾" × 5¾" (7 cm × 12 cm)

MATERIALS FOR THE STOCKING

1 sheet of 8½" × 11" (21.5 cm × 28 cm) card stock for the card base

Felt, as needed

1 button ⅜" (1 cm) in diameter

MATERIALS FOR THE SNOWMAN

1 sheet of 8½" × 11" (21.5 cm × 28 cm) card stock for the card base

Felt, as needed

INSTRUCTIONS

1. Cut each card base to card size.

2. Temporarily attach the template to the card base using masking tape, and cut the design through the template.

3. Score the fold lines by tracing with the tip of a mechanical pencil (without any lead extended).

4. Remove the template, and fold along the scored lines. Keeping the card closed, crease the folds.

5. For the snowman card, attach the muffler-shaped felt cutout using adhesive. Draw the eyes and mouth using a felt-tip pen. For the stocking card, attach the felt and button using adhesive. Write your message using rubber stamps.

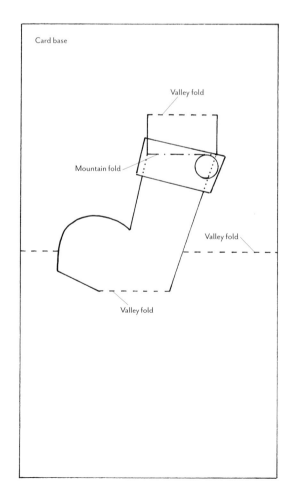

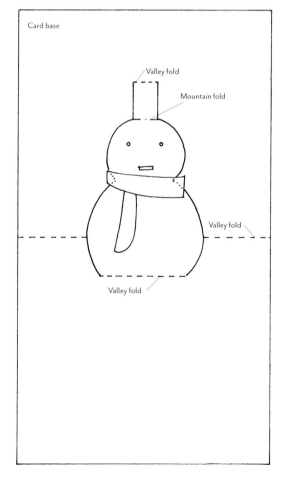

Candelabra

Photograph on page 51

Size: 2¾" × 4" (14 cm × 10 cm)

MATERIALS

2 sheets of 8½" × 11" (21.5 cm × 28 cm) card stock for the card base

1 piece of very thin ribbon 1¾" (4.5 cm) long

INSTRUCTIONS

1. Cut each card base to card size (two pieces, interior and exterior) using a utility knife.

2. Temporarily attach the template to the interior piece using masking tape, and cut the design through the template.

3. Score the fold lines by tracing with the tip of a mechanical pencil (without any lead extended).

4. Turn over the interior piece, and score the fold lines in the same way.

5. Remove the template, and fold along the scored lines. Keeping the card closed, crease the folds.

6. Attach the ribbon using adhesive.

7. Paste the exterior card base to the back of the interior piece.

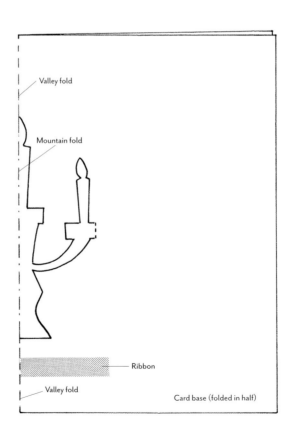

Valley fold

Mountain fold

Ribbon

Valley fold

Card base (folded in half)

Snowflake

Photograph on page 51

Size: 8⅝" × 4⅜" (22 cm × 11 cm)

MATERIALS

1 sheet of 8½" × 11" (21.5 cm × 28 cm) tracing paper for the card base exterior

1 sheet of 8½" × 11" (21.5 cm × 28 cm) Canson Mi-Teintes paper for the card base interior

6 lace snowflakes

INSTRUCTIONS

1. Cut each card base to card size.

2. Temporarily attach the template to the card base interior using masking tape, and cut out the design through the template.

3. Score the fold lines by tracing with the tip of a mechanical pencil (without any lead extended).

4. Turn the card base over, and score the fold lines in the same way.

5. Remove the template, and fold along the scored lines. Keeping the card closed, crease the folds.

6. Attach the lace snowflakes to each side using adhesive.

7. Paste the exterior tracing paper to the back of the interior piece.

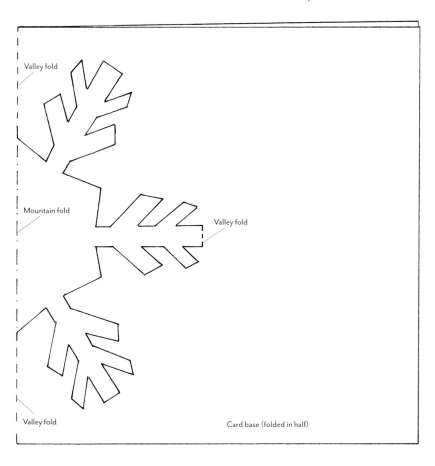

Valley fold

Mountain fold

Valley fold

Valley fold

Card base (folded in half)

Petite Hearts

Photograph on page 53

Size: 4" × 3½" (10 cm x 9 cm)

MATERIALS

3 sheets of 8½" × 11" (21.5 cm × 28 cm) card stock for the card base

3 pieces of fabric 1½" × 1½" (4 cm × 4 cm) each

INSTRUCTIONS

1. Cut each card base to card size.

2. Temporarily attach the template to the card base using masking tape, and cut slits through the template.

3. Score the fold lines by tracing with the tip of a mechanical pencil (without any lead extended).

4. Turn over, and score the fold lines in the same way.

5. Remove the template, and fold along the scored lines. Keeping the card closed, crease the folds.

6. Attach the fabric cut in a smaller heart shape using adhesive.

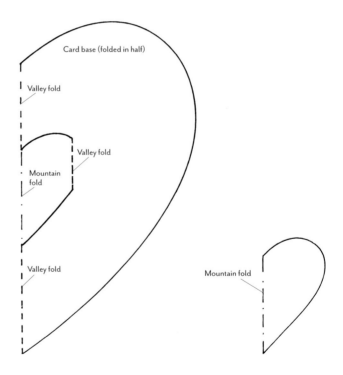

Heart Surprise

Photograph on page 54

Card motifs on page 140

Size: 6¼" × 3⅜" (16 cm × 8.5 cm)

MATERIALS

1 sheet of 8½" × 11" (21.5 cm × 28 cm) card stock for the card base

Color photocopies of the card motifs (small and large hearts)

INSTRUCTIONS

1. Cut the card base to card size.

2. Temporarily attach the template to the card base using masking tape, and cut the design through the template.

3. Trace the position of the end of the coil with the tip of a mechanical pencil (without any lead extended).

4. Temporarily attach the coil template to the leftover card stock, and cut out the design. Remove the template.

5. Apply glue to the tip of the coil, and attach the coil at the position traced on the card base.

6. Apply glue to the center of the other tip of the coil; close the card, and press down to attach the coil.

7. Open the card, and attach the color photocopies of the small and large hearts using paste.

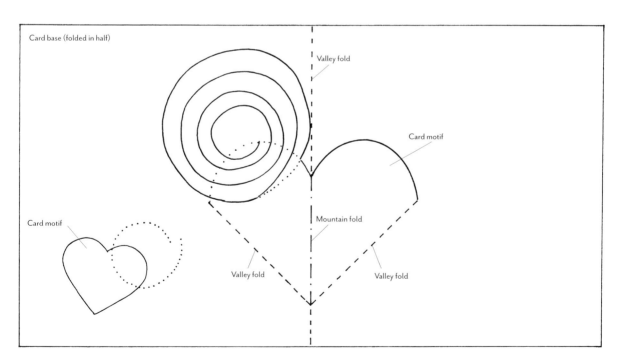

Card base (folded in half)

Valley fold

Card motif

Mountain fold

Card motif

Valley fold

Valley fold

Birds Bearing Happiness

Photograph on page 55

Card motif on page 140

Size: 6¼" × 3½" (16 cm × 9 cm)

MATERIALS

2 sheets of 8½" × 11" (21.5 cm × 28 cm) card stock for the card base

Color photocopies of card motifs (heart and birds' wings)

INSTRUCTIONS

1. Cut each card base to card size (two pieces, interior and exterior) using a utility knife.

2. Temporarily attach the template to the card base using masking tape, and cut the design through the template.

3. Score fold lines by tracing with the tip of a mechanical pencil (without any lead extended).

4. Turn over, and score fold lines in the same way.

5. Remove the template, and fold along the scored lines. Keeping the card closed, crease the folds.

6. Paste on color photocopies of the heart and birds' wings.

7. Paste the exterior card base to the back of the interior piece.

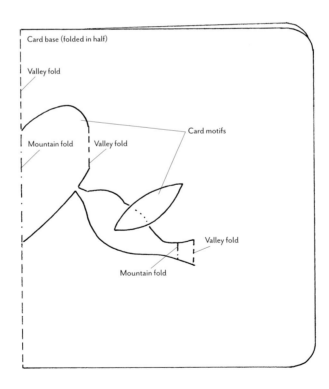

Cracker

Photograph on page 56

Card motifs on page 140

Size: 5" × 4" (13 cm × 10 cm)

MATERIALS

1 sheet of 8½" × 11" (21.5 cm × 28 cm) card stock for the card base

Color photocopies of the card motifs (cracker and confetti)

INSTRUCTIONS

1. Cut the card base to card size.

2. Temporarily attach the template to the card base using masking tape, and cut the design through the template.

3. Score fold lines by tracing with the tip of a mechanical pencil (without any lead extended).

4. Turn the card over, and score fold lines in the same way.

5. Remove the template, and fold along scored lines. Keeping card closed, crease the folds.

6. Paste in place the photocopies of the cracker and confetti.

7. Write your message using rubber stamps.

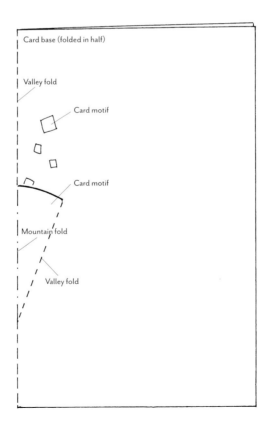

Card base (folded in half)

Valley fold

Card motif

Card motif

Mountain fold

Valley fold

Clover

Photograph on page 57

Card motifs on page 140

Size: 3½" × 5½" (9 cm x 14 cm)

MATERIALS

1 sheet of 8½" × 11" (21.5 cm × 28 cm) watercolor paper for card base

Floral wire 2¾" (7 cm) long

Color photocopies of card motifs (clover, clover with ladybug, and message tags)

INSTRUCTIONS

1. Cut the card base to card size.

2. Temporarily attach the template to the card base using masking tape, and score lines through the pattern.

3. Score the fold lines by tracing with the tip of a mechanical pencil (without any lead extended).

4. Remove the template, and fold along the scored lines. Keeping card closed, crease the folds.

5. Attach the color photocopies of the clover, clover with ladybug, and message tags using paste, and attach the wire using adhesive.

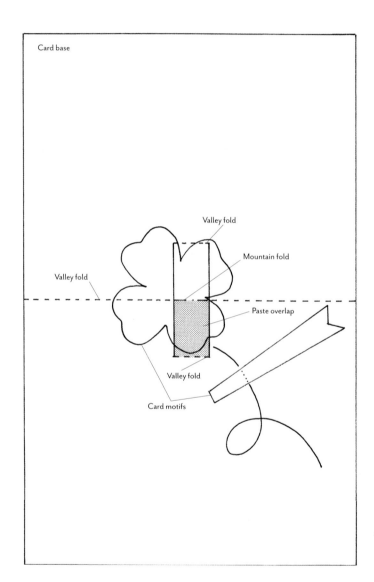

Fluffy Sheep

Photograph on page 58

Size: 8⅝" × 2⅜" (22 cm × 6 cm)

MATERIALS

1 sheet of 8½" × 11" (21.5 cm × 28 cm) card stock for the interior card base

1 sheet of 8½" × 11" (21.5 cm × 28 cm) Canson Mi-Teintes paper for the exterior card base

Raw wool roving or felt, as needed

INSTRUCTIONS

1. Cut each piece of paper to card size.

2. Temporarily attach the template to the interior piece using masking tape, and cut the design through the template.

3. Score fold lines by tracing with the tip of a mechanical pencil (without any lead extended).

4. Remove the template, and fold along the scored lines. Keeping the card closed, crease the folds.

5. Attach the raw wool roving or felt using adhesive.

6. Paste the exterior Mi-Teintes paper to the back of the interior piece.

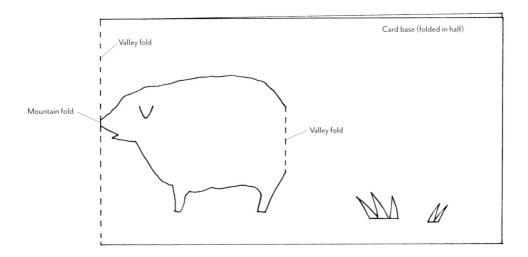

Squirrels in Love

Photograph on page 59

Size: 3½" × 5" (9 cm × 13 cm)

MATERIALS FOR THE SUMMER SQUIRREL (LEFT)

1 sheet of 8½" × 11" (21.5 cm × 28 cm) card stock for the card base

1 sheet of 8½" × 11" (21.5 cm × 28 cm) colored paper

1 piece of felt for the squirrel, 2" × 2" (5 cm × 5 cm)

3 pieces of felt for the tree and heart, 1⅛" × 1⅛" (3 cm × 3 cm) each

MATERIALS FOR THE WINTER SQUIRREL (RIGHT)

1 sheet of 8½" × 11" (21.5 cm × 28 cm) card stock for the interior card base

1 sheet of 8½" × 11" (21.5 cm × 28 cm) colored paper for the exterior card base

1 piece of felt for the squirrel, 2" × 2" (5 cm × 5 cm)

3 pieces of felt for the tree and heart, 1⅛" × 1⅛" (3 cm × 3 cm) each

INSTRUCTIONS

1. Cut each piece of paper to card size.

2. Temporarily attach the template to the interior card base using masking tape, and score lines through the pattern.

3. Score fold lines by tracing with the tip of a mechanical pencil (without any lead extended).

4. Remove the template, and fold along the scored lines. Keeping the card closed, crease the folds.

5. Attach felt cut-outs of the squirrel, heart, and tree using adhesive.

6. Paste exterior colored paper to the back of the card stock.

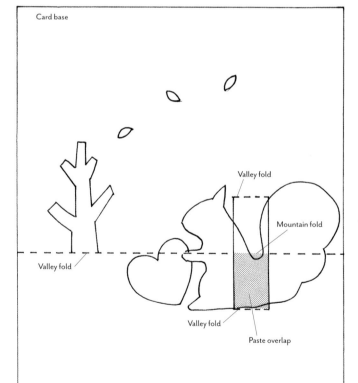

Card base

Valley fold

Mountain fold

Valley fold

Valley fold

Paste overlap

Chapel of Love

Photograph on page 60

Size: 3¾" × 3½" (12 cm × 9 cm)

MATERIALS

1 sheet of 8½" × 11" (21.5 cm × 28 cm) card stock for the interior card base

1 sheet of 8½" × 11" (21.5 cm × 28 cm) colored paper for the exterior card base

1 piece of ½" (1.5 cm) wide lace ribbon, 4¾" (12 cm) long

INSTRUCTIONS

1. Cut each piece of paper to card size (two pieces, interior and exterior) using a utility knife.

2. Temporarily attach the template to the interior piece using masking tape, and cut the design through the template.

3. Score the fold lines by tracing with the tip of a mechanical pencil (without any lead extended).

4. Remove the template, and fold along the scored lines. Keeping the card closed, crease the folds.

5. Paste the exterior colored paper to back of the card stock.

6. Attach lace ribbon along the top edge of the card exterior using adhesive.

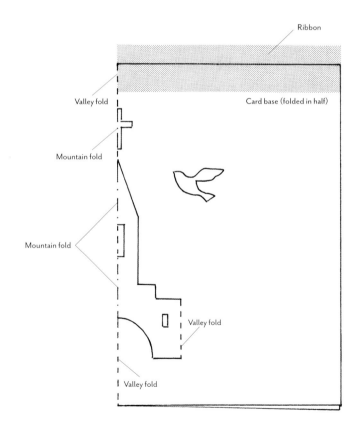

Just Married

Photograph on page 61

Card motifs on page 140

Size: 2¾" × 10¼" (7 cm × 26 cm)

MATERIALS

1 sheet of 8½" × 11" (21.5 cm × 28 cm) card stock for the card base

1 sheet of 8½" × 11" (21.5 cm × 28 cm) Canson Mi-Teintes paper for the coils

Color photocopies of the card motifs (flower petals)

INSTRUCTIONS

1. Cut the card base to card size.

2. Temporarily attach the template to the card base using masking tape, and trace the position of the end of the coil with the tip of a mechanical pencil (without any lead extended). Remove the template.

3. Temporarily attach the two coil templates to the Mi-Teintes paper, and cut out each design. Remove the templates.

4. Apply glue to the paste overlap of the first coil, and attach it to the card base.

5. Apply glue to the tip of the first coil, and attach it to the opposite end of the card base. Close the card, and press down to attach the coil.

6. Apply glue to the tip of the second coil, and attach it to the paste overlap on the card base.

7. Apply glue to the tip of the second coil, and attach it to the tip of the first coil. Close the card, and press down to attach the coils.

8. Open the card, and attach the color photocopies of the flower petals using paste.

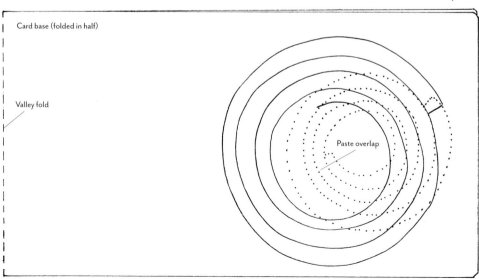

Card base (folded in half)

Valley fold

Paste overlap

Swan

Photograph on page 62

Size: 3⅞" × 6" (10 cm × 15 cm)

MATERIALS

1 sheet of 8½" × 11" (21.5 cm × 28 cm) card stock for the card base

Colored paper for the crown, as needed

1 piece of ½" (1.2 cm) wide beaded ribbon 4" (10 cm) long

INSTRUCTIONS

1. Cut the card base to card size.

2. Temporarily attach the template to the card base using masking tape, and cut the design through the template.

3. Score fold lines by tracing with the tip of a mechanical pencil (without any lead extended).

4. Remove the template, and fold along scored lines. Keeping the card closed, crease the folds.

5. Attach the crown cutout in colored paper using glue, and attach the beaded ribbon using adhesive.

6. Write your message using rubber stamps.

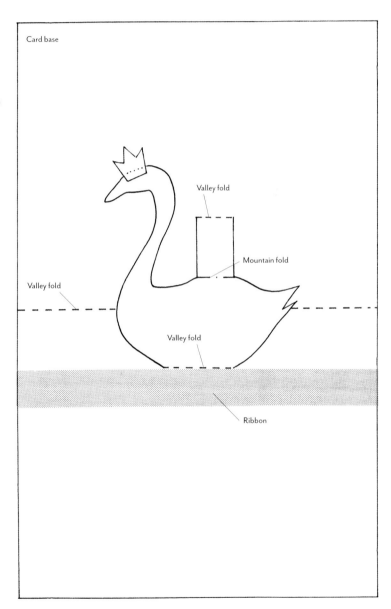

Card base

Valley fold

Mountain fold

Valley fold

Valley fold

Ribbon

First Gift

Photograph on page 62

Size: 8¼" × 3⅛" (21 cm × 8 cm)

MATERIALS

1 sheet of 8½" × 11" (21.5 cm × 28 cm) watercolor paper for the card base

1 piece of Canson Mi-Teintes paper 2⅜" × 3½" (6 cm × 9 cm) for the gift box

1 piece of felt 1⅛" × 1⅛" (3 cm × 3 cm)

1 piece of very thin ribbon 2¾" (7 cm) long

INSTRUCTIONS

1. Cut the card base to card size.

2. Temporarily attach the template to the card base using masking tape, and trace the position where the gift box will be attached with the tip of a mechanical pencil (without any lead extended). Remove the template.

3. Temporarily attach the gift box template to the Mi-Teintes paper, and score the fold lines by tracing them with the tip of a mechanical pencil (without any lead extended).

4. Cut out the gift box.

5. Remove the template, and fold along the scored lines. Apply glue to the paste overlap, and connect the gift box.

6. Apply glue to one of the gift box's triangular paste overlaps, and attach the overlap to the card base. Apply glue to the other triangular paste overlap, and close the card to secure it.

7. Attach the ribbon and felt cutout in bootie shapes using adhesive.

8. Write your message using rubber stamps.

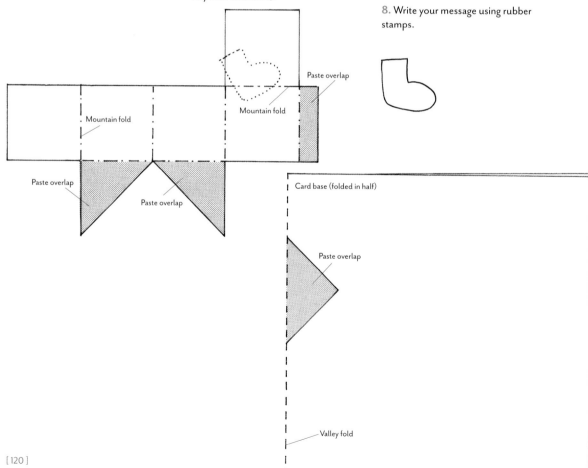

Rocking Horse

Photograph on page 63

Card motif on page 140

Size: 3 ⅛" × 4 ¾" (8 cm × 12 cm)

MATERIALS

1 sheet of 8½" × 11" (21.5 cm × 28 cm) watercolor paper for the card base

1 piece of 1 ⅜" (3.5 cm) wide lace ribbon 3 ⅛" (8 cm) long

Color photocopy of card motif (rocking horse)

INSTRUCTIONS

1. Cut the card base to card size.

2. Temporarily attach the template to the card base using masking tape, and score lines through the template.

3. Score fold lines by tracing with the tip of a mechanical pencil (without any lead extended).

4. Remove the template, and fold along scored lines. Keeping the card closed, crease the folds.

5. Attach the lace ribbon and a color photocopy of the rocking horse using paste.

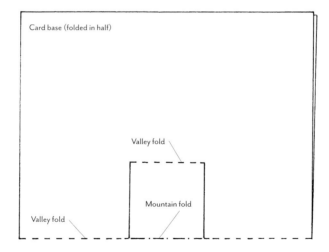

Card base (folded in half)

Valley fold

Mountain fold

Valley fold

Penguin on an Ice Floe

Photograph on page 66

Instructions on page 67

Card motifs on page 141

Size: 6 ⅜" × 6" (16 cm × 15.5 cm)

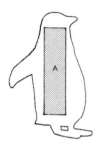

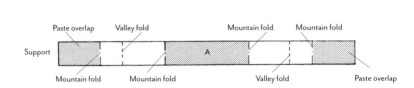

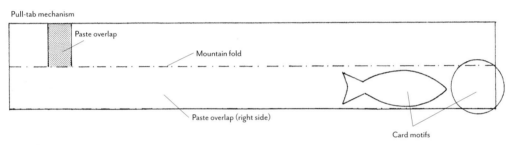

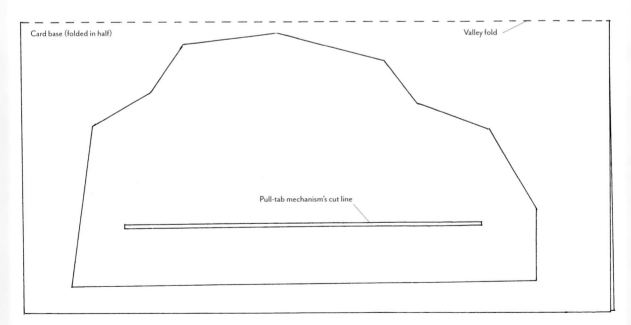

Hungry Kitty

Photograph on page 68

Instructions on page 69

Card motifs on page 141

Size: 4" × 5½" (10 cm × 14 cm)

Fold line

Pull-tab mechanism

Paste overlap

Mountain fold

Paste overlap

Mountain fold

Paste overlap

Paste overlap (right side)

Card base (folded in half)

Paste overlap
(right side)

Card motifs

Mountain fold

Pull-tab mechanism's cut line

Pull-tab
mechanism's
cut line

Paste overlap
(right side)

Mountain fold

Card motifs

Sheepherding Dog

Photograph on page 70

Card motifs on page 141

Size: 6¼" × 6" (16 cm × 15.5 cm)

MATERIALS

1 sheet of 8½" × 11" (21.5 cm × 28 cm) card stock for the card base

1 sheet of 8½" × 11" (21.5 cm × 28 cm) card stock for the mountain and the pull-tab mechanism

Canson Mi-Teintes paper for the dog and support, as needed

Color photocopies of the card motifs (sheep and trees)

INSTRUCTIONS

1. Cut one piece of card stock to card size.

2. Temporarily attach the mountain template to the other piece of card stock, and cut out the mountain. Remove the template.

3. Temporarily attach the pull-tab template to the leftover card base, and score fold lines by tracing with the tip of a mechanical pencil (without any lead extended). Cut out the pull-tab, and remove the template. Fold along scored line, and glue together.

4. Temporarily attach the dog and support template to the Mi-Teintes paper, and score the fold lines by tracing with the tip of a mechanical pencil (without any lead extended). Cut out the dog and support.

5. Remove the template, and fold along the scored line of support. Apply glue to the paste overlap, and connect the support. Apply glue to the back of the dog, and attach it to the support.

6. Apply glue to the support, and attach the pull-tab mechanism through the bottom.

7. Paste color photocopies of the sheep on the pull tab, and paste trees on the mountain.

8. Insert the dog into the line of the mountain's pull-tab mechanism from behind.

9. Apply glue all around the edges of the mountain (except where pull-tab mechanism sticks out), and attach to the card base.

10. Pull on the tab mechanism, and adjust as needed.

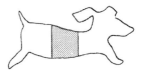

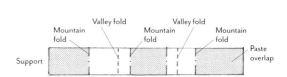

Support

Mountain fold

Valley fold

Valley fold

Mountain fold

Mountain fold

Mountain fold

Paste overlap

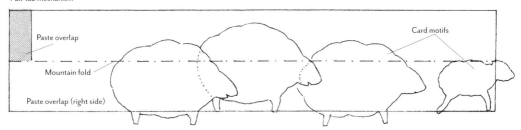

Pull-tab mechanism

Paste overlap

Card motifs

Mountain fold

Paste overlap (right side)

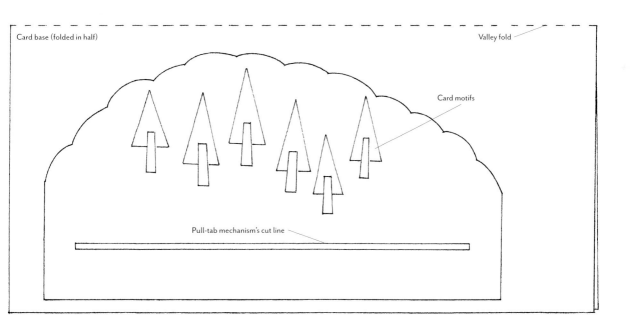

Card base (folded in half)

Valley fold

Card motifs

Pull-tab mechanism's cut line

Love Bunny

Photograph on page 71

Card motifs on page 141

Size: 9½" × 3⅛" (24 cm × 8 cm)

MATERIALS

1 sheet of 8½" × 11" (21.5 cm × 28 cm) card stock for the card base

1 sheet of 8½" × 11" (21.5 cm × 28 cm) Canson Mi-Teintes paper for the heart

Color photocopies of the card motifs (bunny and heart)

INSTRUCTIONS

1. Cut the card base to size A (9½" × 3⅛" [24 cm × 8 cm]) and size B (4¾" × 3⅛" [12 cm × 8 cm]).

2. Temporarily attach the template to card base B, and cut out a slit for the pull-tab mechanism through the template. Remove the template.

3. Temporarily attach the pull-tab template to the leftover card base. Score the fold lines by tracing them with the tip of a mechanical pencil (without any lead extended), and cut out the pull tab using a utility knife.

4. Remove the template, and fold along the scored line. Apply glue to paste overlaps to secure the pull tab.

5. Temporarily attach the heart-shaped mechanism template to Mi-Teintes paper. Score fold lines by tracing with the tip of a mechanical pencil (without any lead extended), and cut out using a utility knife. Remove the template.

6. Insert the pull-tab mechanism into the slit of the card base.

7. Paste the heart-shaped mechanism to the pull-tab mechanism by sandwiching it around the tab's narrowed tip.

8. Turn over card base B, and fold the pull-tab mechanism along fold lines.

9. Using paste, attach the color photocopies of the bunnies, and attach the heart to the end of the pull-tab mechanism.

10. Paste the exterior card base A to the back of card base B. Write your message using rubber stamps.

11. Pull on the tab mechanism, and adjust as needed.

Paste overlap

Card motif

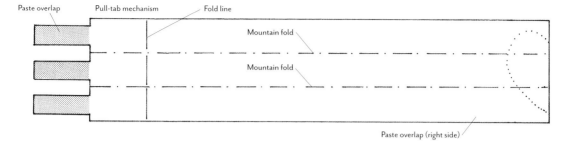

Paste overlap   Pull-tab mechanism   Fold line

Mountain fold

Mountain fold

Paste overlap (right side)

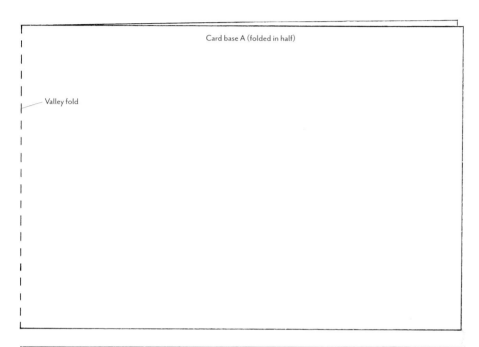

Card base A (folded in half)

Valley fold

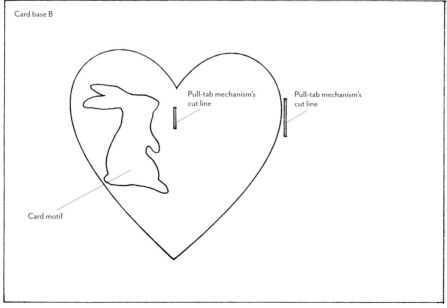

Card base B

Pull-tab mechanism's
cut line

Pull-tab mechanism's
cut line

Card motif

Soap Bubbles

Photograph on page 72

Instructions on page 73

Card motifs on page 141

Size: 4¼" × 4" (11 cm × 10 cm)

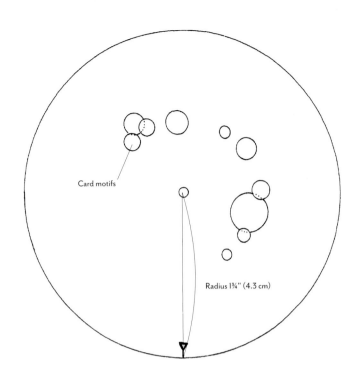

Card motifs

Radius 1¾" (4.3 cm)

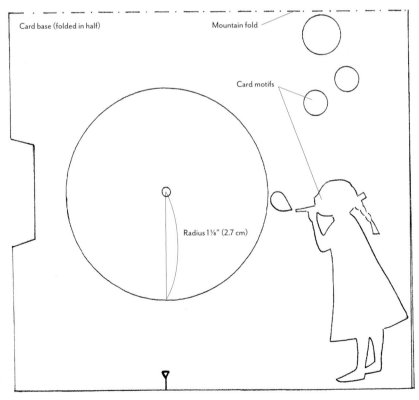

Card base (folded in half)

Mountain fold

Card motifs

Radius 1⅛" (2.7 cm)

Dahlia

Photograph on page 74

Card motif on page 142

Size: 3½" × 3½" (9 cm × 9 cm)

MATERIALS

1 sheet of 8½" × 11" (21.5 cm × 28 cm) Canson Mi-Teintes paper for the card base

1 split pin

Color photocopy of card motif (spiral pattern)

INSTRUCTIONS

1. Cut the card base to size A (7" × 3½" [18 cm × 9 cm]) and size B (3½" × 3½" [9 cm × 9 cm]).

2. Temporarily attach the template to card base B using masking tape, and cut the design through the template.

3. Place the circle template on the leftover paper, and cut a circle with a radius of 1¾" (4.3 cm) using a circle cutter.

4. Remove the circle template, and paste in place a color photocopy of the spiral pattern. Mark the center of the circle using a mechanical pencil.

5. Place card base B over the circle, and align the circles' centers. Make a hole in the center using an awl.

6. Insert the split pin into the hole, and fasten it from the other side.

7. Apply glue to the four corners of card base B, and paste it to the exterior card base A.

8. Write your message using rubber stamps.

Card base A (folded in half)

Valley fold

Radius 1¾" (4.3 cm)

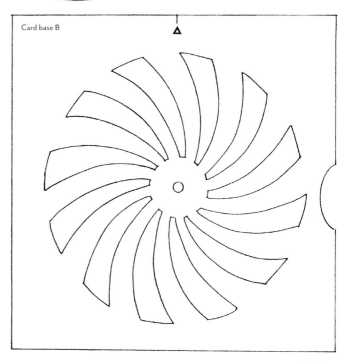

Card base B

Circus Elephant

Photograph on page 75

Card motifs on page 142

Size: 2¾" × 6¼" (7 cm × 16 cm)

MATERIALS

1 sheet of 8½" × 11" (21.5 cm × 28 cm) Canson Mi-Teintes paper for the card bases

Canson Mi-Teintes paper for the elephant, as needed

Colored paper, as needed

1 split pin

Color photocopies of card motifs (ball and flags)

INSTRUCTIONS

1. Cut card base A and card base B to card size.

2. Temporarily attach the template to card base B using masking tape, and cut a circle with a radius of ¾" (1.8 cm) using a circle cutter.

3. Remove the template. Mark the center of the circle using a mechanical pencil.

4. Temporarily attach the circle template C to the leftover paper, and cut a circle with a radius of 1⅜" (3.5 cm) using a circle cutter.

5. Remove the template, and mark the center of the circle using a mechanical pencil. Attach a color photocopy of the ball motif using paste. Cut slits on circle template C.

6. Fold the card base B in half, and insert the circle in between. Align the circles' centers. Make a hole in the center using an awl.

7. Insert the split pin, and fasten it from the other side.

8. Temporarily attach the elephant template to a piece of Mi-Teintes paper, and cut it out. Insert the paste overlaps into both slits in the larger circle. Apply glue to the surface of the paste overlaps, and attach them to the back of the circle.

9. Apply glue to the four corners of the back of card base B, and attach it to card base A.

10. Attach the color photocopy of the flags using paste. Write your message using rubber stamps.

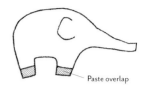

Paste overlap

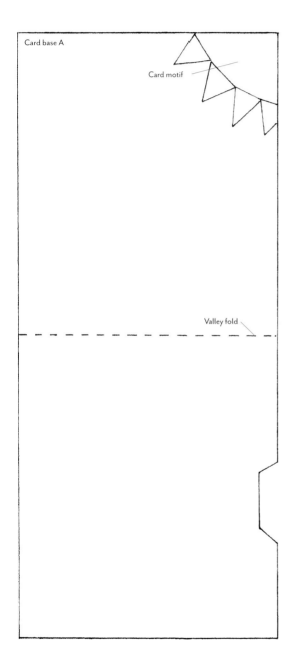

Card base A

Card motif

Valley fold

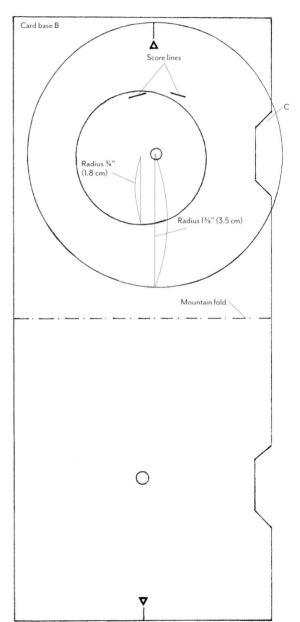

Card base B

Score lines

C

Radius ¾"
(1.8 cm)

Radius 1⅜" (3.5 cm)

Mountain fold

Hopping Bunny

Photograph on page 76

Instructions on page 77

Card motif on page 142

Size: 9½" × 3½" (24 cm × 9 cm)

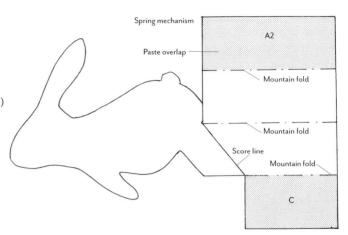

Spring mechanism

Paste overlap

A2

Mountain fold

Mountain fold

Score line

Mountain fold

C

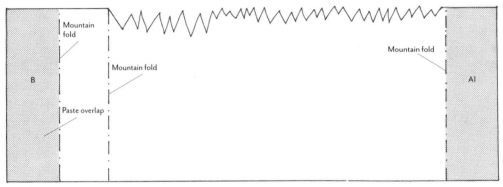

Mountain fold

Mountain fold

Mountain fold

Paste overlap

B

A1

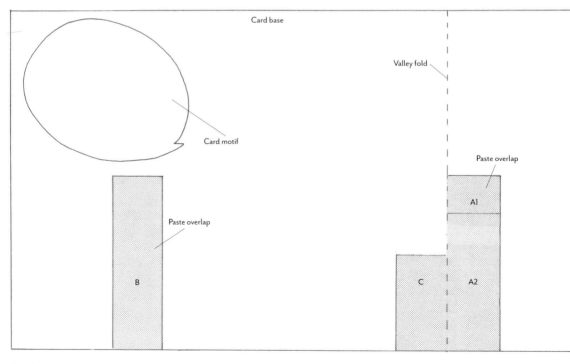

Card base

Valley fold

Card motif

Paste overlap

Paste overlap

A1

B

C

A2

Magic Show

Photograph on page 78

Size: 8½" x 4½" (22 cm x 11.5 cm)

MATERIALS

1 sheet of 8½" × 11" (21.5 cm × 28 cm) card stock for the card base

¼ sheet of 8½" × 11" (21.5 cm × 28 cm) card stock for the hat

¼ sheet of 8½" × 11" (21.5 cm × 28 cm) card stock for the dove

1 piece of very thin ribbon 1⅜" (3.5 cm) long

INSTRUCTIONS

1. Cut the card base to card size.

2. Temporarily attach the template to the card base using masking tape, and trace the paste overlap with the tip of a mechanical pencil (without any lead extended). Remove the template.

3. Temporarily attach the table template to the leftover paper. Score the fold lines, tracing with the tip of a mechanical pencil (without any lead extended), and cut out using scissors. Remove the template.

4. In the same way, temporarily attach the top hat and dove templates to the respective paper, and cut them out.

5. Fold the spring mechanism along the fold lines.

6. Attach using paste the right end of what will become the table to the paste overlap on the card base.

7. Attach using paste the right end of the spring mechanism to the same paste overlap.

8. Attach the left end of the spring mechanism using paste.

9. Fold the table to cover the spring mechanism, and paste down the other side.

10. Pull out the tab of the spring mechanism from underneath the table, and attach the dove using paste. Replace and adjust so that the dove cannot be seen when hidden under the table.

11. Attach the ribbon to the top hat using adhesive. Use a cotton swab to make the silver dot pattern.

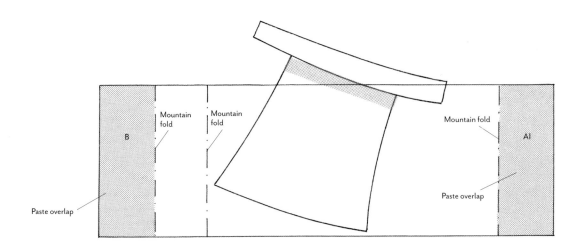

B

Paste overlap

Mountain
fold

Mountain
fold

Mountain fold

A1

Paste overlap

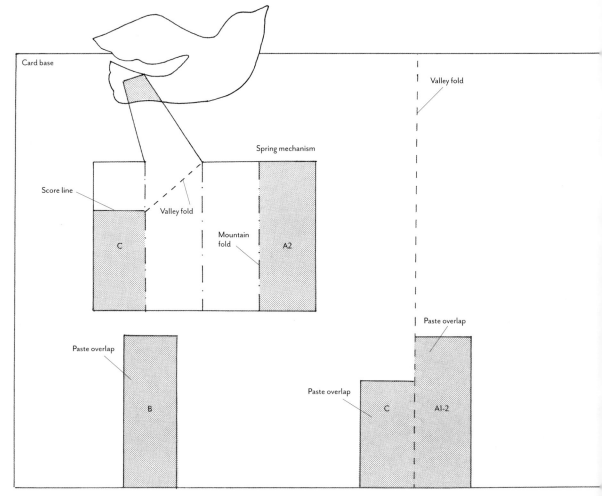

Card base

Valley fold

Spring mechanism

Score line

Valley fold

C

Mountain
fold

A2

Paste overlap

Paste overlap

B

Paste overlap

C

A1-2

Paste overlap

Birthday Wishes

Photograph on page 79

Card motifs on page 142

Size: 8¼" × 3½" (21 cm × 9 cm)

MATERIALS

1 sheet of 8½" × 11" (21.5 cm × 28 cm) card stock for the card base

1 sheet of 8½" × 11" (21.5 cm × 28 cm) card stock for the interior pieces

1 piece of ½" (1.5) cm wide lace ribbon 2½" (6.5 cm) long

Color photocopies of card motifs (cake and gift box)

INSTRUCTIONS

1. Cut the card base to card size.

2. Temporarily attach the template to the card base using masking tape, and trace the points of attachment with the tip of a mechanical pencil (without any lead extended). Remove the template.

3. Temporarily attach the table template to the card stock. Score the fold lines, tracing with the tip of a mechanical pencil (without any lead extended), and cut out using scissors. Remove the template.

4. Temporarily attach the message template to the leftover card stock. Trace the points of attachment with the tip of a mechanical pencil (without any lead extended), and cut out using scissors. Remove the template. Attach the lace ribbon using adhesive, and write your message using rubber stamps.

5. Temporarily attach the spring mechanism template to the leftover card stock. Score the fold lines, and trace the points of attachment with the tip of a mechanical pencil (without any lead extended), and cut out using scissors. Remove the template. Fold the spring mechanism along the fold lines.

6. Use paste to attach the right end of what will become the table to the paste overlap on the card base.

7. Use paste to attach the right end of the spring mechanism to the same paste overlap.

8. Attach the left end of the spring mechanism using paste.

9. Fold the table to cover the spring mechanism, and paste down the other side.

10. Pull out the tab of the spring mechanism from underneath the table, and attach the birthday-message card using paste.

11. Attach the color photocopies of the cake and gift box using paste.

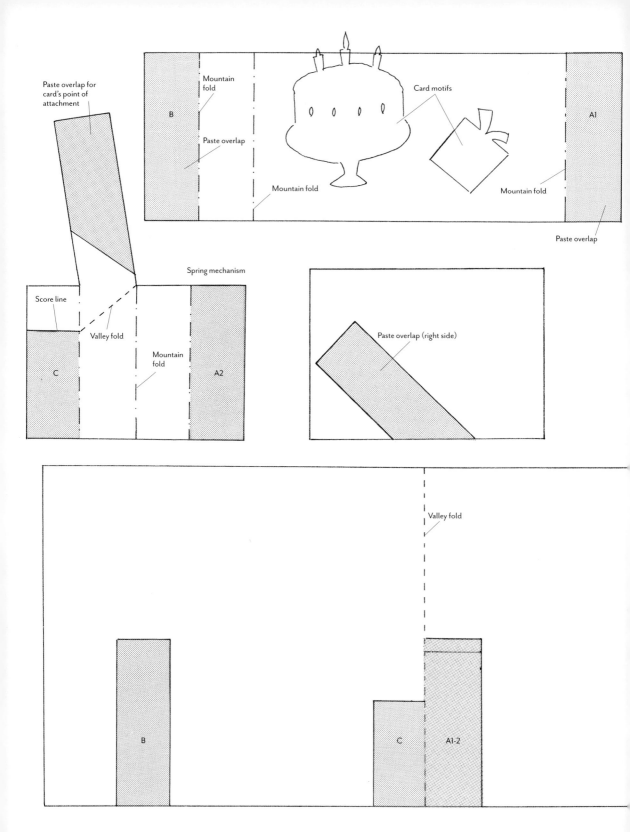

Paste overlap for card's point of attachment

Mountain fold

B

Paste overlap

Mountain fold

Card motifs

A1

Mountain fold

Paste overlap

Spring mechanism

Score line

Valley fold

C

Mountain fold

A2

Paste overlap (right side)

Valley fold

B

C

A1-2

Color Card Motifs

Make color photocopies of the following card motifs, and then cut them out using scissors or a utility knife and paste them onto your cards. All designs are full size.

page 15 Ballerina Dancing Onstage

page 18 Parisian Scene

page 20 Raindrops

page 22 Teatime

page 23 Three Sisters

page 24 Spring's Arrival

page 26 Sweethearts

page 27 The North Wind and the Sun

page 30 Happy Halloween

page 31 Woodland Friends

page 32 Strawberry Basket

page 34 Rabbit in the Briar

page 40 Special Delivery Present

page 41 Birthday Cake

page 41 Bouquet

page 49 Wintry Mountain Deer

page 54 Heart Surprise

page 55 Birds Bearing Happiness

page 57 Clover

page 56 Cracker

THANK YOU!

HELLO!

page 61 Just Married

page 63 Rocking Horse

page 66 Penguin on an Ice Floe

page 68 Hungry Kitty

page 70 Sheepherding Dog

page 71 Love Bunny

page 72 Soap Bubbles

page 74 Dahlia

page 75 Circus Elephant

page 76 Hopping Bunny

page 79 Birthday Wishes

About the Author

A craft book author and illustrator, Mari Kumada has a particular fancy for being surrounded by pretty papers—wrapping paper, stamps, bookmarks, and the like. She got her start at *Hand & Heart* (Benesse Corporation), where she oversaw the magazine's features on handmade craft goods such as *sashiko* embroidery, appliqué, claywork, and so on. Kumada is the author of *First Kirigami Lessons* (Shufunotomo) and the co-author of *Fun with Pipecleaners* (Ondori), *Cute Kirigami Lessons* (Shufunotomo), and *Colorful Accessories* (Ondori), among others.

An imprint of Shambhala Publications, Inc.
Horticultural Hall
300 Massachusetts Avenue
Boston, Massachusetts 02115
roostbooks.com

Copyright © 2008 Mari Kumada
Translation © 2012 by Shambhala Publications, Inc.
Translated by Allison Markin Powell

Staff
Art Direction & Design: Mihoko Amano
Design (Instructions): Keiko Iehara
Stylist: Akiko Suzuki
Photography: Tomoe Ueda, Mitsuru Chiba,
Emiko Suzuki, Kazunori Shibata (Processing by
Shufunotomo Co. Photo Studio)
Models: Konan, Ruka
Editor: Shino Nishimura
In-house editor: Takashi Shinoaki (Shufunotomo)

All rights reserved. No part of this book may be
reproduced in any form or by any means, electronic
or mechanical, including photocopying, recording,
or by any information storage and retrieval system,
without permission in writing from the publisher.

9 8 7 6 5 4 3 2 1
First English Edition
Originally published in Japan in 2008 by
Shufunotomo Co., Ltd. as *Kawaii Pop-Up Card*
by Mari Kumada. World English translation rights
arranged with Shufunotomo Co., Ltd. through
The English Agency (Japan) Ltd.

Printed in China

♾ This edition is printed on acid-free paper that
meets the American National Standards Institute
Z39.48 Standard.

♻ Shambhala makes every effort to print on
recycled paper. For more information please visit
www.shambhala.com.

Distributed in the United States by Random House,
Inc., and in Canada by Random House of Canada Ltd

Designed by Gopa & Ted2, Inc.

Library of Congress Cataloging-in-Publication Data

Kumada, Mari.
Pop-up cards: over 50 designs for cards that fold,
flap, spin, and slide / Mari Kumada.
p.   cm.
ISBN 978-1-61180-004-3 (pbk.: alk. paper) 1.
Greeting cards. 2. Paper work. 3. Cut-out craft. I.
Title.
TT872.K86 2012
745.594'1—dc23
2011042330